GLADIATOR

PHILIP MATYSZAK

GLADIATOR

THE ROMAN FIGHTER'S
UNOFFICIAL MANUAL

114 illustrations, 22 in color

HALF TITLE *A hoplomachus and a Thracian doing weapons drill.*
TITLE PAGE *Brutus Britannicus Thrax, the baby-eating Barbarian,
invites you to a bit of unfriendly stab-and-slash.*

First published in 2011 in hardcover in the United States
of America by Thames & Hudson Inc., 500 Fifth Avenue,
New York, New York 10110

thamesandhudsonusa.com

Library of Congress Catalog Card Number 2010935686

ISBN 978-0-500-05167-2

Designed and typeset by Fred Birdsall Studio
Printed and bound in China by Toppan Leefung Printing Limited

Contents

Becoming a Gladiator

If anyone can do it, believe that you can too.
MARCUS AURELIUS *MEDITATIONS* 6.19

✛ ✛ ✛

Welcome to the world of the gladiator, a strange world full of con-tradictions. This is where the dishonoured learn to live and die with honour. Here, the artist is as despised as his art is respected; and in turn many gladiators scorn the spectators at the arena, but yet are dying – sometimes literally – to entertain them. This manual will take the reader from the first faltering steps over the threshold of gladiator school, and through training to become a 'man of the sword' (which is what *gladiator* literally means). Then on to mastery of the arcane art of arena combat – who knows, perhaps in the presence of the emperor himself – and finally to retirement, though this last chapter may be redundant for some.

For the right kind of person the arena offers riches, fame and personal redemption, and even the wrong kind of person gets the chance of an hon-ourable death. And anyone considering a gladiatorial career is probably well aware that worse things can happen. In fact many gladiators choose the profession precisely because those worse things would otherwise happen to them in the near future.

- -

Rome's new emperor dressed to go clubbing. As his un-imperial attire shows, Commodus is a fan of Hercules and of violent combat sports in general.

Picture yourself under this helmet. Yes – you too can become a gladiator of Rome and fight in the arena! All it takes is hard work, training and a lot of bad luck.

On the bright side, there has never been a better time to be a gladiator. For centuries, gladiatorial bouts have steadily become more popular, and the crowds ever larger and more enthusiastic. In this year, AD 180, the emperor Marcus Aurelius of blessed memory has just passed away and his son and successor Commodus is well known to be mad about gladiators. (Or perhaps just mad, but that's not the point.) The important thing is that gladiatorial combat is about to enter a golden age, and someone with the appropriate qualifications can be right at the cutting edge of developments. Cast aside your doubts, for fame and fortune await!

A job like no other

The nice thing about becoming a gladiator is that you are no longer alone in a harsh, uncaring world. Not only are there now people who care whether you live or die, but they care intensely, and often stake large amounts of money on one of these two outcomes.

By definition the gladiator is a misfit, an outcast for one reason or another rejected by Roman society. Life for those excluded from the benefits of Roman civilization can be rough. So while the glamour of the arena draws some to a gladiatorial career, most are motivated by desperation, and the lack of any viable alternative. By and large, a gladiator is someone who has taken the job after running through several other careers, possibly including bandit, beggar, mugger, cattle rustler or failed professional gambler. Once the authorities close in, a mid-career switch to becoming a gladiator can be the chance of a lifetime, albeit in the sense that it is the only chance of still having a lifetime. The Romans do not believe in rehabilitation in the community, and becoming a gladiator is often the best of some truly terrible options.

✛ ✛ ✛

Those who hire themselves out to the arena pay for their food and drink with their blood.

SENECA *LETTERS* 37

✛ ✛ ✛

- - - - - - - - - - - - - - - - - - - -
Having a leopard eat your face is one of the alternatives that makes being a gladiator seem an attractive prospect. (See Damnatio ad bestias, *opposite.) This charming detail comes from a mosaic in a Roman house in El Djem, Tunisia.*

So how does one become a gladiator?

1 Be an unsuccessful (and preferably violent) criminal

Judges belong to the elite in their society, and as such participate in the trade in favours that greases the wheels of Roman administration. The giving of games in the amphitheatre is a duty (*munus*) of many provincial officials, and these officials will be duly grateful for participants referred to them by the courts. In Rome itself the emperor personally presents arena spectacles. Imperial games are larger and more sensational than provincial offerings, and the number of positions vacant is correspondingly higher.

✣ ✣ ✣

Gladiators are either foredoomed men or barbarians…
CICERO *TUSCULAN DISPUTATIONS* 2.41

✣ ✣ ✣

Although the slave mines or crucifixion, for example, are also options for sentencing, the judge may temper justice with what the *munerarius* – a presenter of the games – has in mind and the manpower required for the execution of it. A judge sending a criminal to the arena may choose one of the following sentences:

Damnatio ad bestias The *munerarius* has procured some large carnivores at great expense, and rather than risk the beasts being damaged in the arena he will display them as they rip the condemned into bloody chunks. Therefore a sentence of *damnatio ad bestias* is very bad news. The criminal has missed the chance to be a gladiator and instead becomes one of the *noxi*, those without hope of salvation.

Damnatio ad gladium This is marginally better, though still fatal. It means that the condemned is sentenced to die by the sword (*gladius*), but if he looks as if he can wield one entertainingly, he might be allowed a sword of his own as well. Sometimes the condemned is sentenced to fight as a gladiator, but with the stipulation that he must be dead within a year or two.

Damnatio ad ludos Condemned to the games. For the right type, this might mean that a career as a gladiator beckons. Being condemned to the arena and being condemned to death are not the same thing, and with energy and ambition, and a not inconsiderable slice of luck, the outcome can be made to be altogether different.

✛ ✛ ✛

There is a distinction between those sentenced to the sword and those sentenced to the games, for the former die straight away, or at most within a year.

MODESTINUS *THE DIGEST OF JUSTINIAN* 48.19.31

✛ ✛ ✛

You are a filthy gladiator, who after murdering your host, escaped by pure luck from the criminals' cage at the amphitheatre!

INSULT FROM PETRONIUS *SATYRICON* 9

✛ ✛ ✛

2 Lose a war against Rome

In AD 180 the Roman empire and its army are near their peak, so losing to the Romans is not difficult. After his accession in 161, Marcus Aurelius campaigned successfully in Parthia and Germany and his subordinates are still fighting minor actions in Africa, Britain and around the Black Sea. All of these campaigns bring back hordes of prisoners of war, many of them already trained in the use of arms and therefore natural arena fodder. In fact, several types of gladiator are already named after warriors who fought in their native style after being captured by the Romans in past wars.

- -

For this captured barbarian warrior the war may be over, but the fighting has just begun. A legionary leads a captive off to his new life, in a bas-relief from the Arch of Diocletian in Rome.

✛ ✛ ✛

When the enemy surrendered, Aquillius ordered that they be spared
immediate execution and took them to Rome to fight there…

CASSIUS DIO *HISTORY* 36.10
(ON THE FATE OF SICILIAN REBELS IN 100 BC)

✛ ✛ ✛

This part of the spectacle used up a great many British captives…

CASSIUS DIO *HISTORY* 60.30

✛ ✛ ✛

3 Be a surly and recalcitrant slave

Many who fall into this category started in category #2 and simply discovered that subservience was not in their nature. The penalty for actually striking one's owner is unlikely to leave an unruly slave fit for the arena, but a general disposition to violence might be enough to send him there. Note that a court of law must consent to the sale of slaves for lethal amphitheatre appearances, and this includes selling someone off to become a gladiator.

✛ ✛ ✛

[The emperor Hadrian] prohibited the selling of a male or female
slave to a brothel or a lanista without the seller having first made a
case for his conduct.

HISTORIA AUGUSTA: *LIFE OF HADRIAN* 18

✛ ✛ ✛

4 Owe more money than you can repay

Some people sell themselves. Rome has little sympathy for debtors. Indeed, the Twelve Tables, the foundation stone of Roman law, suggest that if a period of imprisonment fails to produce the goods a creditor can literally carve his pound of flesh off the debtor. In these more civilized times, it is likelier that the assets of the debtor will be sold to repay the debt, and the person of the debtor is one of his assets. Nor is it unknown for a creditor, once he has received his former debtor as a slave, to torture him (as he is now perfectly entitled to do) to check that nothing further of value has been squirrelled away from his grasp.

And this is merely what the law permits. Some debt collectors are less sensitive to an individual's civic rights. Indeed, many who voluntarily sign up for the arena originally* got the idea from the gladiators hired to forcibly collect their debt.

In short, it is better to sell oneself than wait for someone else to do it for you – with physical violence thrown in as a non-optional extra.

✦ ✦ ✦

There was competition among country towns in Italy to offer the highest enticements to get truly degraded young gentlemen to fight [in the arena].
TACITUS *HISTORIES* 2.62

✦ ✦ ✦

5 Decide to commit social suicide

✦ ✦ ✦

Everything he did that was coarse, foul, cruel or typical of a gladiator.
HISTORIA AUGUSTA: LIFE OF COMMODUS 13.3

✦ ✦ ✦

Those who voluntarily sign on as gladiators are called *auctorati*, in that they are the authors of their own misfortunes. The perverse glamour of gladiatorial combat sometimes inspires otherwise respectable young males – and even the occasional respectable female – to yearn to participate in the fights in the arena. It is shocking and unacceptable for a lady to appear on public display for any reason whatsoever, so the young woman's yearning must remain unrequited. However, for males a distinction is made between men who appear in the arena *quaestus causa* – i.e. fighting for the money – and

---

* Once they recovered from the beating

those who do so *virtus causa* – to show off their martial ability. Who knows, even the emperor Commodus might appear *virtus causa*. He is certainly (gladiator-) mad enough to try.

A fighter who performs *virtus causa* is socially frowned upon, but almost acceptable, especially if he modestly selects a helmet that guarantees a degree of anonymity. However, anyone who fights purely for money, especially if he signs on with a gladiator school beforehand, is *infamis*, or officially scum. An *infamis* cannot vote, hold public office or even procure a decent burial plot. No decent person will have social relations with an *infamis* for fear of being considered one himself, so becoming a gladiator is an irrevocable step. There is no going back, ever, which is exactly why some rebellious sons (often to their enduring regret) do so to defy their parents or a former lover.

✛ ✛ ✛

*He was neither a criminal nor forced to the arena by the adversity of
fortune. Gentlemen, he became a gladiator as a display of virtus.*

QUINTILIAN *DECLAMATIONS* 16

✛ ✛ ✛

*While for the Greeks there is no shame to go onstage and present oneself
to the public gaze, for us [Romans] this thing is considered infamous and
humiliating – the opposite of honourable.*

CORNELIUS NEPOS *LIVES* 5 (PREFACE)

✛ ✛ ✛

6 Step up from the gutter

Not everyone who becomes a gladiator has any social standing to lose. Country boys with excellent physiques who have come to Rome with the idea of making their fortunes rapidly lower their sights to merely making a living. They then discover this can only be done in a brothel or the arena, and some opt for the latter.

Then there are ex-soldiers who have managed to blow their pensions on the wrong woman or on ill-advised betting on the Blues in the chariot races. If signing on for another 25 years in the legions has no appeal, the shorter contracts offered by gladiator schools may be an attractive alternative to men with no other skills. This is especially true for soldiers who have received a *missio ignominiosa*, or dishonourable discharge from the army, as they start as *infames* in the first place.

7 Be a woman or a dwarf with fighting skills

Editores – as those who organize the games are called – are always on the lookout for something new to present in their spectaculars. Amphitheatre crowds are blasé about the sight of death, eager for novelty and appreciative when they get it. Therefore a *nanus* (i.e. a psychopathic killer of reduced growth) is very welcome in these politically incorrect times. Meanwhile, those rare women with a decent ability for swordplay will find the *ludus* (see below) an eager equal-opportunity employer, especially of those who do not inquire too deeply into the nature of the opportunity.

Finding a gladiator school (*ludus*)

There is such a thing as a freelance gladiator, but these are established names who have to be lured out of retirement for one-off performances. The luring usually involves amounts of gold that leave younger gladiators breathless with disbelief and envy, and quite often involves pressure from some highly connected individuals as well. For example, when the emperor Tiberius wanted some famous gladiators to appear in spectacular games in his grandfather's memory, the price of bringing them out of retirement was 100,000 *sestertii* a fighter, which is enough to keep a poor family going for several centuries.

Tiberius liked to give gladiatorial shows, but he punished the people of Pollentia when they demanded one, and he passed legislation limiting the number of gladiatorial pairs that could fight in a single show.

✝ ✝ ✝

He's young, tempestuous and capable of serving in the army. But the gossips say that without the tribune's sanction or prohibition he'll sign himself away to some tyrannical lanista and take the gladiator's oath.

JUVENAL *SATIRES* 11.6-8

✝ ✝ ✝

No such option is available to those starting on a gladiatorial career. For an *auctoratus* a basic salary might be negotiated when he joins the school, but those who arrive involuntarily from the courts get no such privileges. And even the *auctoratus* will find that once his food, bedding, training and incidental medical expenses have been paid, he is little better off than his colleagues in the unfree labour force which makes up more than half of the complement of most gladiator schools.

Nevertheless, it is important to select a *ludus* with great care. (Note that even quite large towns might not have gladiator schools, so finding one that fits his needs may require some travelling on the part of the aspiring gladiator.) Of course all such schools are supervised by the imperial government's office of *procuratores familiae ludi*, for the very obvious reason that any sensible government will want to oversee the activities of large bodies of men training in the use of deadly weapons. In the *Satyricon* of Petronius there is a reference to a wealthy landholder who had enough gladiators 'to plunder Carthage', and indeed some of the bigger schools have hundreds, if not thousands, of fighters on their rolls.

Imperial supervision aside, quality of life and frequency of death varies greatly depending on the type and quality of the *ludus* in question. Here are some of the options:

The imperial schools

Back in the dying days of the Republic, Julius Caesar was the first to realize that he could save a fortune (literally) by having his own gladiator schools instead of hiring gladiators for each occasion. Others followed his example, for owning gladiators was almost as prestigious as being their manager (*lanista*) was disgraceful. Thus Cicero once complimented his friend

Atticus on acquiring a school so prestigious that it would repay the purchase price as soon as it had been hired out once or twice. Caesar's heir, Augustus, inherited several thousand gladiators as part of his patrimony, and these schools, now moved from Campania to Rome, are today part of the imperial estate.

Ever the showman, Caesar combined practicality with crowd-pleasing by keeping his own schools of gladiators. The Roman Senate was so worried by the number of armed men under Caesar's control that they passed legislation limiting the number of gladiators that could be used in a public display.

Pros

1 The imperial schools are the best *ludi* in the business
2 They have the best doctors to patch up salvageable losers
3 Their trainers are highly skilled
4 You get to live in Rome
5 You may appear before the emperor himself at the Colosseum
6 The rewards are potentially huge

Cons

1 You generally fight others from your *ludus*, and they too have had excellent training
2 Emperors can afford a high wastage rate in their gladiatorial complement
3 Colosseum crowds are harder to please and eager for blood

The gladiator's workplace. The oval of the amphitheatre – this is the one at Colonia Nemausus (Nimes) – brings the spectators intimately close to the action. A gladiator only appears here three or four times a year – the rest of the time is spent doing intensive training. There's nowhere to hide in the amphitheatre, and a high price for failure.

- - - - - - - - - - - - - - - - - - -

A provincial school

Though not every amphitheatre comes with its own *ludus*, there's an amphitheatre in every major city in the empire. No one has counted them all, but there are about 200 of sufficiently respectable size that no first-rate gladiator would be embarrassed to appear there. However, local fame counts for a lot in this business, so few top gladiators are interested in fighting on other than their home ground. The ownership and prestige of provincial schools may vary, but often the chief contractors who pay for the games are priests of the imperial cult who lay on the spectacles in the emperor's name. Some local grandees with political ambitions may also try to buy votes in this highly traditional way, but games featuring a significant number of gladiators require permission from imperial officials.

Some cities may have their own municipal *ludus*, while other *ludi* are owned by a private party. Generally this is a local aristocrat who works in tandem with a retired gladiator, but who keeps his partner at arm's length, because a retired gladiator is still a gladiator and an *infamis*.

Pros	Cons
1 A smaller school and a better chance to know your opponent's weaknesses	1 A smaller school and a better chance that your opponent will know your weaknesses
2 Easier to build up a fan base	2 Less chance of becoming disgustingly rich and famous
3 Lower probability of fatal combats	3 Inferior doctors

A travelling show

These obscure bands, often featuring a few discharged soldiers and a reformed bandit or two, can be found traipsing from market to market, generally performing 'exhibition' shows, since at this level actually losing someone in a combat is a financial and personal disaster for the often tightly knit troupe. Therefore fights tend to be highly staged affairs more reminiscent of the theatre than the arena. Expect withering scorn or at least pitying patronage from any 'real' gladiators.

✛ ✛ ✛

[The slave] Asiaticus behaved so insolently and so thievishly that Vitellius sold him to the lanista of a travelling gladiator show.

SUETONIUS *LIFE OF VITELLIUS* 12

✛ ✛ ✛

Pros	Cons
1 It's marginally better than banditry or acting for those with no talent for either	1 The feeling you are at the bottom of the ladder
2 You get to see the world outside the *ludus*	2 The incidental risks of travel
3 Hopefully any vegetables thrown at you will be fresh	3 Claustrophobia of working with the same small group
4 You probably won't die on the sand of the arena – not least because your arenas can't afford sand	4 Poverty

Someone in a position to make a choice as to which of the above is preferable is almost certainly – for the moment – a free person. Before signing away one's liberty, it is highly advisable to do some more research. First, and perhaps surprisingly, not everyone is welcome at a gladiator school. Every *ludus* has a reputation to maintain, and producing inferior gladiators in the arena is the surest way to destroy that reputation and with it the livelihoods of everyone in the school. A condemnation such as the one below might be the death-knell for a school if it was generally believed:

✢ ✢ ✢

*And when you get down to it what has he ever done for us? He gave a
show of two-bit gladiators! They were such a rickety lot that if you'd blown
on them, they'd have fallen flat on their faces…He killed his mounted
men by torchlight, and you might have taken them for dunghill cocks. One
was mule-footed, another bandy-legged, while the third, put up to replace
a dead man, was a dead weight himself, because he was hamstrung before
the fight started. The only one who made any effort was a Thracian,
and he only fought when we forced him to. In the end they all got a sound
thrashing; in fact the crowd booed every one of them, and they were
blatantly runaway [slaves].*

PETRONIUS *SATYRICON* 45

✢ ✢ ✢

*A trainee auditions as a gladiator, using items of cast-off kit. His
lower body stance is good, though his upper body posture is too
defensive. Training can eliminate technical flaws, but timidity
is a fatal weakness.*

A gladiator is a valuable item of property who needs weeks, if not months,
of careful training before a good *lanista* will consider putting him up for an
arena performance. This costs a considerable sum of money, and there is
not a lot of point in making the effort for someone who will bring more dis-
repute than honour on the *munerarius* who presents the games. Therefore,
select a school that seems likely to accept you, and then:

• Get clearance from your local magistrate. The state needs to be assured
that any free person signing as a gladiator does so voluntarily, and has a
physique that at least offers him a hope of survival.

• Check the reputation of the prospective school carefully. A school that
will take new gladiators with no questions asked is a school one needs
to ask a lot of questions about. It might be a school with a very high
turnover of personnel, which from a tiro's perspective is not good news.

- Observe the behaviour of gladiators while they are outside the *ludus*. Do they seem brutalized and cowed? (If the gladiators are kept imprisoned within the *ludus*, they are either condemned criminals or being treated as such. Avoid.)

- Get inside information. It's a rare gladiator who will refuse a drink, so try talking to one on the neutral ground of a tavern before going for a more formal interview at the school itself.

- Above all, try to watch the gladiators of a potential school in action in the arena, taking careful note of the treatment of the defeated and the size of the prize for the victor. (Gladiator shows happen only rarely, so someone with urgent debts to repay might not have this luxury.)

Gladiators at work, shown in a frieze from Pompeii. Anyone signing up to a gladiator school should be prepared for ungentle treatment. Gladiators work hard and play rough. Expect bullying and brutal initiation rites as soon as you step through the door.

Signing up and swearing in

Only when certain that school and candidate are right for each other should a potential gladiator present himself to the *lanista* in charge. After an assessment, which may or may not involve a brief trial bout in the training ring, the potential gladiator receives either a rejection or an offer of a place.

For an *auctoratus*, this offer may include a cash payment for his body, for make no mistake – joining a gladiator school means selling oneself, body and soul, to that school.

The key terms to seek during negotiation are 4,000 *sestertii* and four or five years. The former is a legal minimum value that is put on your body should you die in the arena, and usually 2,000 *sestertii* are paid directly to the *auctoratus* when he signs up. Without this valuation a new recruit might end up as a *gregarius*, one of those gladiators who fight in packs until one or the other group is wiped out, or be thrown away in a crowd-pleasing but lethal spectacle. It is unlikely that the candidate will be able to negotiate how many times a year he appears in the arena. Without provision or exception, even if he enters as a free man, once he has been sworn in a gladiator is the property of the *lanista* to be disposed of as he thinks fit. The number of years is important, because anyone surviving four or five years is generally released from their contract.

✣ ✣ ✣

Like free-born gladiators selling our liberty, we religiously devoted
both soul and body to our new master.

PETRONIUS *SATYRICON* 117

✣ ✣ ✣

Think long and hard before accepting a place in a *ludus*. Acceptance involves swearing the *sacramentum gladiatorum* – the infamous gladiator's oath. Even those gladiators condemned to die in the arena take this oath. In swearing, they replace the sentence of the court with a voluntary doom that they have 'freely' accepted for themselves. For the condemned, the gladiator's oath offers a form of redemption, allowing them to substitute an honourable death by the sword for a dishonourable death as a condemned criminal. All the same, a free man who swears the oath remains only technically free (and an *infamis*), for he has handed himself into servitude, voluntarily becoming little better than the condemned wretches alongside whom he will train and fight.

To take the oath, both *auctorati* and condemned criminals proclaim before witnesses that they give over their bodies to their new master to be 'burned, flogged, beaten or slain by cold steel, as their owner should order'. Once the oath has been sworn, you are formally a member of the *ludus*, one of the *tirones* or beginners. Although at the very bottom of the ladder, you are nevertheless officially a gladiator.

Congratulations are definitely not in order.

Codex Gladiorum

Feeding the arena is not hard. In his Jewish campaign of AD 69–70 Titus took 97,000 prisoners, many of whom finished up in the arena, either for straightforward execution or to fight as gladiators.

✜

Crucifixions seldom happen in the amphitheatre, as the process takes too long to be entertaining.

✜

✜

When Caligula was ill, a man made an oath to fight in the arena if the emperor recovered. Caligula held the man to his word, and watched the swordplay intently until the man won his fight and begged abjectly to be released from his vow.

- - - - - - - - - - - - - - - -

ABOVE *Gaius Caligula, who occasionally agonized about gladiators being more popular with the masses than he was.*

A member of Rome's noble Gracchus clan forever disgraced himself by fighting as a net-man in the arena, where everyone could see his face. Even worse, he put on a pathetically cowardly display.

✜

There is some dispute as to whether gladiators or actors are at the bottom of Roman society, but according to the orator Calpurnius Flaccus, 'no one of the people is lower than a gladiator'.

✜

A *munerarius* contemplating the cost of a particularly magnificent show can apply to the courts for a supply of condemned prisoners to take part in various events.

✜

Those breaking a gladiatorial oath become *sacer*, or liable to summary execution to appease the god whom the oath-breaker has offended.

✜

The word 'arena' comes from the latin *harena*, or 'sand', as this covers the floor of the fighting area.

✛ II ✛
How Did We Get Here?

It's about how you live, not about how long you live.

SENECA *LETTERS* 101.15

✛ ✛ ✛

et's face it – having people fight and kill each other for entertainment requires some pretty flexible moral gymnastics before it's palatable to anyone with a conscience. The stern old Romans of the early Republic were not in the least averse to a bit of cruelty and bloodshed. But until the very end, they tended to kill people out of necessity and not for sport. For hundreds of years, while the Romans conquered Italy and fought Hannibal, gladiatorial combats were limited and rare. The Greeks were initially somewhat shocked by the idea, though they have lately been raising their own amphitheatres with enthusiasm.

So how did we reach the present situation, where tens of thousands of gladiators are in training, and thousands of them die every year in arenas custom-built for the purpose? This question is sometimes raised by the dinner-party set, as shown by the quotations below from Athenaeus's work *The Dinner of the Wise* (*The Deipnosophists*).

Blame the Etruscans

The Etruscans as a people are gone now, totally absorbed into the fabric of Roman society, and even their language is extinct. But those who feel uneasy about the 'sport' of gladiatorial combat can still pin the blame on that mysterious people.

✦ ✦ ✦

The Romans put on exhibitions in which gladiators fought…a custom they borrowed from the Etruscans.

ATHENAEUS *THE DEIPNOSOPHISTS* 39

✦ ✦ ✦

A case to support Athenaeus can be made from the following points:

- There was something decadent and oriental about the Etruscans, just as there is something about gladiatorial combat that jars slightly with the Romans' image of themselves as straightforward, no-nonsense, frank, disciplined, manly types.

- This ancient Etruscan race were a bit uncanny. Even today, many of Rome's religious practices and superstitions are based on Etruscan rites. And do not some gladiators carry into the arena an amulet allegedly made in some arcane Etruscan ritual that offers protection from evil spirits, shielding from harm, or just general good luck?

- As Roman gladiators originally fought, and presumably died, at funeral games, and as this is as close to an institution of human sacrifice as the Romans got, it is evident the idea must have come from outside.

- Did not the Etruscans sacrifice humans to the spirits of the deceased? And were gladiatorial combats in Rome not originally a part of the funeral rites for great men? So the Romans adopted the Etruscan tradition of gladiatorial games just as they adopted the Etruscan tradition of chariot racing.

- It's a fact that in 356 BC, in the early days of the Republic, the Etruscans sacrificed 307 Roman prisoners of war to their gods. And so even now, in Rome, there is a religious aspect to the killing of prisoners of war in the arena. Obviously, one can see where Rome got the idea.

- At the Roman games, a fallen gladiator may be given the coup de grâce by a hammer-bearing individual impersonating the underworld deity Dis Pater. This character bears an uncommon resemblance to Charun, the hammer-bearing divinity who appears in the background of many a gory Etruscan fresco.

So it makes sense to claim that gladiatorial combat is an Etruscan tradition that has somehow polluted the Roman consciousness.

Blame the Campanians

Of course the Etruscans are not the only ones responsible. A patriotic Roman can also blame the Campanians. Campania is an area south of Rome, and the Campanian settlements of Capua and Caere were among the first major cities to fall to the expansionist power of Rome. The area was long dominated by the Samnites, a proud and stubborn people whom it took the Romans several centuries to bring fully under control. In fact as recently as 90 BC it looked for a while as though

ABOVE *Charun Psychopompus, guide of the dead. This character has been adapted for the Roman arena and uses his hammer to finish off the mortally wounded. He is the last thing many arena victims see before dying, and if the Etruscans are right, the first thing they see afterwards.*

RIGHT *Samnite warriors as the Roman legions saw them, from a tomb painting at Paestum of the 4th century BC.*

Rome was actually going to end up under Samnite dominion. It can be argued that the Campanians gave the Romans the idea of gladiatorial combat because:

- It is known that long before the Romans got the idea, duels between individuals were fought in the arenas of Campania for the delectation and edification of spectators. Even now some very ancient Campanian buildings have frescoes that show couples engaged in what looks very much like gladiatorial combat, and these frescoes date from a time when the practice was unknown in Rome.

- It's no coincidence that the first arenas for gladiator fights were built in Campania, and many Campanian cities had substantial stone-built arenas before the first one was even contemplated in Rome.

- It is very probable that captured Roman soldiers were made to fight as gladiators. It is also likely that the Romans promptly did the same right back to their captured Samnites. (In the same spirit of reciprocity, after the Etruscans sacrificed the 307 Romans, the Romans took 368 of their noblest Etruscan captives and flogged and beheaded them in the forum.)

- Is not the very oldest of Roman gladiator types called the 'Samnite', and is that not because of the very events described above?

- The conclusive argument – before it was captured by the Samnites, Capua was an Etruscan city. Need we say more?

Anyone else?

✢ ✢ ✢

Hermippus in Book I of his Lawgivers says that the Mantineans [in Greece] originally came up with the idea of gladiator fights, having been given the idea by Demonax, one of their citizens.

ATHENAEUS *THE DEIPNOSOPHISTS* 4.40
(DEMON-AX. WHAT A GREAT NAME FOR A GLADIATOR!)

✢ ✢ ✢

Actually, blame the Romans

Sadly for those who would love to prove that gladiators were an outside influence, which corrupted the true Roman spirit (as no doubt many will argue in future ages to justify their own idealized version of Rome), all of the above points are easily refuted.

- If the Romans simply inherited the practice from the Etruscans, why is the first mention of gladiatorial combat only in 264 BC, and described by Livy as an exceptional event? A genuinely Etruscan tradition, chariot racing, was openly part of Rome's culture from the beginning. Did gladiatorial combat somehow lurk unnoticed and undiscovered in the fabric of Rome for half a millennium before it burst into the open?

A chariot race at the Circus Maximus. Chariot racing is an Etruscan import that is almost more popular than gladiator fights.

- Roman gladiatorial duels originally had the pretext of honouring the spirit of the dead, but they rapidly diverged from this concept, so that gladiator exhibitions were soon tied much more closely to the electoral cycle of aspiring politicians than to the lifespan of the deceased being honoured.

- In Etruscan human sacrifice, the victims were dedicated to a particular god and killed for that purpose – the fact that they sometimes died in combat was incidental to the sacrifice. In Rome, the religious element is only involved because in Rome there is a religious element to everything, but particularly to the passing of a human life, even if that life is felt to be slightly sub-human.

Where it all started? This bronze basrelief from the side panel of a 6th-century BC *chariot shows two Etruscan warriors in single combat.*

- The tradition of the duel is at least as old as Homer, and good for a few millennia yet. There is no reason to assume that the single combats of Campania and the Samnites were not duels, rather like those of the Celts described by Athenaeus in another passage:

✛ ✛ ✛

On occasion the Celts may also have single combats at their entertainments…if the bystanders do not stop them, [the participants] go so far as to kill one another.

ATHENAEUS *THE DEIPNOSOPHISTS* 4.40

✛ ✛ ✛

It is more probable that gladiator combats in Rome were originally displays by powerful men who wanted to show that they could have people fight and die at their command and for their entertainment. Some Etruscan religious trappings were used as a fig leaf to cover this abuse of naked power, but the wellspring of enthusiasm for gladiator combat is found, not in any attempt to commune with the divine, but in the Roman desire for visible and total dominance over others.

The fact is that there never was and never will be a phenomenon like the contemporary gladiator, who is so uniquely Roman that he might as well have 'MADE IN ROME' branded across him in large letters. Undoubtedly the Romans picked up some of the ideas involved in gladiatorial combat from other cultures, just as they have copied – and improved – so much else. For better or worse, like the purple-cloaked emperor and the iron-clad legionary, the gladiator on the sands of the arena has become one of the eternal symbols of imperial Rome.

From funeral entertainer to arena superstar – a brief biography of the Roman gladiator

264 BC   Enter the gladiator

The very first recorded combat of gladiator pairs took place in Rome. The historian Livy recorded the occasion in a brief aside, saying that in this year 'Decimus Iunius Brutus put on the first display of gladiators as a tribute to honour his deceased father'.

The actual words used were *munus gladiatorium*. A *munus* means a duty, or an obligation of honour, which in this case Decimus Brutus fulfilled by using gladiators. Exactly what happened is now lost in the mists of time, but two or three pairs of condemned criminals may have fought to the death at the site where Brutus senior was laid to rest. The analogy Brutus probably used was that of Achilles, the hero of the Trojan war, who sacrificed captured prisoners on the grave of his friend Patroclus.

✛ ✛ ✛

The first gladiatorial games were held in the Forum Boarium [between the Circus Maximus and the Tiber] in the consulship of Appius Claudius and Marcus Fulvius.

VALERIUS MAXIMUS 2.4.7

✛ ✛ ✛

216 BC *The start of the arms race*

One Aemilius Lepidus was seen off into the afterlife with a *munus* laid on by his sons, which featured 22 pairs of gladiators. From hints in the historical tradition we can assume that gladiators had become a regular feature of aristocratic funerals by this time, but it seems that in 216 BC the Aemilius boys raised the bar for everyone else. Being highly competitive, no Roman aristocrat would stage games with a lesser number of gladiators and admit his inferior resources. So, every time the number of gladiators in a *munus* went up, this became the new standard. In 166 BC, Titus Flamininus presented 37 pairs at his father's funeral games.

206 BC *Not at funerals*

Scipio Africanus put on games in honour of his father and uncle, killed in Spain during the ongoing Second Punic War. This is significant because Scipio's father and uncle had died half a decade before. This marks the increasing separation of a *munus* from the death it was ostensibly commemorating.

166 BC *Going Greek*

Seeing the popularity of gladiator shows in Rome, the Hellenistic monarch Antiochus Epiphanes staged games of his own. Antiochus was ruler of the Seleucid empire, and his games took place in Antioch in Syria, the city named after his line. This may have been seen on the Greek mainland as another sad example of the Seleucids 'going barbarian', but it wasn't much longer before the Greeks were building amphitheatres of their own. In 69 BC gladiatorial combats took place in Ephesus, a Greek city in Asia Minor [see p. 40].

✛ ✛ ✛

And this same king [Antiochus Epiphanes] when he heard of the games staged in Macedonia by Aemilius Paulus the Roman general, wanted to surpass Paulus in his magnificence and liberality and arranged for…240 pairs of gladiators to fight in single combat.

ATHENAEUS *THE DEIPNOSOPHISTS* 5.22

✛ ✛ ✛

121 BC   Games without barriers

✛ ✛ ✛

A show of gladiators was to take place in the forum. The presiding officials put up scaffolding around the event, so that they could rent out the seating. Caius commanded them to take this down so that the poor people could see the event for free.

PLUTARCH *LIFE OF CAIUS GRACCHUS* 12.3
(WHEN THE OFFICIALS DID NOT LISTEN, GRACCHUS BROUGHT A
GANG OF WORKMEN AND DEMOLISHED THE SCAFFOLDING HIMSELF)

✛ ✛ ✛

105 BC   Going mainstream military

Rome was fighting for its life against a huge wave of barbarian invaders in the north of Italy. The consul Rutilius Rufus hit upon the idea of using trainers from gladiator schools to train his infantry. (Which tells us that by then a substantial number of gladiator schools were up and running.) The troops trained in this way were so effective that Caius Marius, who was consul after Rufus, preferred them to his own conventionally trained soldiers. Later, Marius tried to pretend that training with gladiators was his idea all along.

It was at this time, if not earlier, that the Romans started encouraging their soldiers to go regularly to watch gladiator fights, not only so that they might appreciate the finer points of swordplay, but also to get them accustomed to the sight of people dying violently by the sword.

73 BC   Spartacus

In 73 BC Spartacus started with a band of escaped gladiators, which grew to an army that plundered Italy from top to bottom and back again in a two-year rampage. Slave revolts were not unknown to the Romans. The brutal conditions on the farms of Sicily caused large-scale slave rebellions – mostly starting on the huge estates of absentee Roman landlords. These erupted more frequently than nearby Mount Etna, and with even more disastrous consequences. But until the growth of the gladiator phenomenon, the Romans did not have to worry that the hard core of the revolt had been meticulously trained to the highest degree in hand-to-hand combat.

Spartacus: Rome's nightmare in the flesh

In the mid-70s BC, Italy was a tinder-box waiting for a spark. There had been repeated food shortages, and bitter resentments remained among the Samnite peoples over their treatment by the Roman dictator after the final failure of their revolt against Rome some 20 years previously. The Roman aristocracy had greedily increased their ancestral estates by pushing poorer peasants off the land, and many soldiers – 'those who fight and die for Rome' as the reformer Tiberius Gracchus put it – ended up with 'nothing but the air of Italy and sunlight of Italy to call their own'.

Enter Spartacus, one of the most controversial and enigmatic figures in Roman history. Little is known about him, not even his real name, for the name we have was given to him by his *lanista* for arena appearances. We do know that he was a criminal sentenced to the arena, perhaps for deserting from the Roman *auxilia*, perhaps for banditry, perhaps for both. We know that he endured a particularly brutal training regime in the *ludus* of one Lentulus Batiatus in Capua. Spartacus led a daring break-out from the school. While fleeing town the gladiators encountered the wagon carrying goods for the forthcoming gladiatorial show, so Spartacus and his men armed themselves with the very armour and weapons with which they were scheduled to fight in the arena.

Spartacus and his fellow gladiators became bandits, with their head-quarters in the crater of what the Romans fondly believed to be the extinct volcano of Vesuvius, overlooking Pompeii. And there, had circumstances been different, he might have dropped out of history.

But Spartacus had a fatal flaw: he was a great leader. In consequence, his gladiator band rapidly acquired other followers – runaway slaves, disaffected ex-soldiers and dispossessed peasants. Eventually he had a small army, which was something the Romans could not ignore. They levied troops against him, and once Spartacus had defeated these, he not only had a large army, but thanks to the weapons and armour of those he had defeated, he also had a well-equipped one.

With his gladiators at the spearhead, Spartacus plundered his way down through Italy, looting not merely farmsteads, but towns and small cities. After a winter preparing his forces, Spartacus went north, defeating Roman army after Roman army, including a veteran force of 10,000 men sent against him from Gaul. When he had broken through to the Alps, and he and his men looked at the mountain passes that led to freedom, the gladiator army turned south once more.

Why they did so, no one can say for certain, but it was a fatal mistake. Spartacus plundered his way through Italy once again, attracting so many recruits that he had to turn them away from his army. However, when he reached the toe of Italy, he was pinned there for a time by the general Marcus Crassus. Spartacus broke out but was eventually defeated by Crassus near the port city of Brundisium. In a splendid piece of theatre, Spartacus killed his horse before the final battle to show that he would not run away. Presumably he died – Plutarch says he was cut down, fighting to the last – but his body was never found.

Statuette of a Thracian gladiator – what Spartacus was originally intended to be.

Spartacus is described as having had an amiable, vaguely 'sheep-like' countenance, but there was nothing sheep-like about his personality. No freedom-fighter he. Spartacus cheerfully enslaved any Romans who resisted him, and was happy to make gladiators of his captives and have them fight to the death for his amusement. In Roman eyes, the disgrace of being repeatedly defeated by an army of those whom they considered human garbage was somewhat mitigated by the fact that, under the leadership of Spartacus, the rebels fought and died like men. The manner of their dying, like that of true gladiators, gave both them and their opponents some degree of honour.

✣ ✣ ✣

That battle was the most hard fought of all. Although his men killed 12,300 men in the fight, only two of these had wounds in the back. The rest held their ranks and died there fighting the Romans.

PLUTARCH *LIFE OF CRASSUS* 11

✣ ✣ ✣

65 BC   Caesar ups the stakes

The ambitious, unscrupulous, and unconventional young politician Julius Caesar decided to offer funeral games for his father. While games and funerals had been taking place ever further apart, eyebrows were raised on this occasion. Though his father had been dead for 20 years, Caesar, currently *aedile*, had ambitions for yet higher political office and his games were a blatant bid for popular support.

These were, of course, no ordinary games. With characteristic extravagance, Caesar presented 320 pairs of gladiators, all in single combats (i.e. no mass brawls of *gregarii*). This was the highlight of a programme that featured public banquets, processions and theatrical events. Unsurprisingly, Caesar won his next election.

65 BC   Gladiators and high politics

At this time there were no standing armed forces in Rome. In fact, even a conquering Roman general had to surrender his command before he could re-enter the city. Therefore Caesar's 640 highly trained fighters represented a small but potent private army, and since many (with justification) suspected that Caesar might try to overthrow the Republic, laws were hastily passed preventing anyone from staging games within two years of seeking high public office.

Other laws were passed soon afterwards, limiting the number of gladiators that could appear at any given event. This was both to limit the number of armed fighters in Rome and to prevent other senators following Caesar's example and going deep into debt to stage public spectacles.

60 BC   Escalating crisis

With the Republic spiralling towards collapse, demagogues used mob rule to get their way. Bloody riots were common in the forum. In fact, Julius Caesar lost a grandson when his pregnant daughter collapsed after seeing her husband Pompey come home covered in (someone else's) blood after one such lively political debate.

In such circumstances, those who could afford it went into the political fray with a coterie of battle-hardened gladiators at their backs, all the better to intimidate the riff-raff.

55 BC   Birth of permanent arenas

Up to this point, entertainment in Rome had always been staged in temporary venues, often in the forum, and without seating, as Republican Romans thought it decadent to sit while enjoying a display. In 55 BC Pompey, now a famous general, used his wealth and prestige to build a permanent theatre.

✢ ✢ ✢

The custom of gladiators fighting in the forum has come down to us from our ancestors.

VITRUVIUS *ON ARCHITECTURE* 5.1
(WRITTEN EARLY IN THE REIGN OF AUGUSTUS)

✢ ✢ ✢

A contemporary politician, Scribonius Curio, constructed two temporary banks of theatre seats back to back on wheels and a pivot. When these two theatres were swivelled so that they came together face to face, the two curving banks of seats formed an oval space that was used for gladiator displays. This ingenious contraption suffered from problems with its construction and soon stopped working (and while it was in operation, those on it were allegedly in more danger than the gladiators), but the oval shape formed between the two theatres has given us the name *amphi* ('two') *theatre*.

53 BC   Death of Clodius

In a fracas on the Appian Way, the retinue of Annius Milo, a candidate for the consulship, was attacked by Publius Clodius of Rome's ancient Claudian line. The 'armed and convicted malefactors' whom Cicero numbers in Clodius's force were almost certainly gladiators, and it is highly probable that Milo had more than a few of his own, since his retinue won and Clodius was killed.

42 BC   State-sponsored gladiatorial games

In response to terrible omens, and to quiet a populace that had become ever more turbulent since the assassination of Julius Caesar, the Roman government for the first time presented gladiator fights as an official event.

22 BC Augustus takes over

As well as instituting the *procurator*'s office mentioned above for the empire-wide control of gladiator schools, in this year Augustus limited the number of gladiators to 60 pairs for all games (though naturally he exempted himself from this provision). He built a relatively modest amphitheatre for gladiatorial bouts. Augustus also separated male from female spectators, perhaps because of activities such as those described by Ovid below:

✛ ✛ ✛

Many a man, who came to see another wounded, finds that he has been smitten himself. While he is talking and stroking her hand... [Cupid's] arrow hits him before he knows what's happening. He sighs deeply and, instead of being a mere spectator to the fight, he finds himself its victim.

OVID *THE ART OF LOVE*
(LATER IN THE SAME POEM, WHEN ADVISING GIRLS ON WHERE TO
PICK UP MEN, HE URGES THEM TO 'GO TO THE ARENA STILL WARM
WITH BLOOD NEW-SHED')

✛ ✛ ✛

AD 27 Horror at Fidenae

✛ ✛ ✛

A certain freedman called Atilius decided to build an amphitheatre at Fidenae for the exhibition of a show of gladiators. He did this neither to show his wealth nor to court public approval, but simply for sordid profit. Consequently he did not make the foundations of the amphitheatre sufficiently solid, nor did he ensure that the wooden superstructure has buttresses of adequate strength...dense crowds had packed the building when it gave a violent shudder and collapsed, falling either inwards or outwards. The multitude who were intently watching *the show either fell or were crushed to death. Those who were crushed to death had at least the advantage of instant death, while others were trapped in the debris, with limbs torn off, listening to their relatives dying…50,000 persons were killed or crippled in this disaster.* The Senate decreed that in future no one worth less than 400,000 sestertii could stage gladiator shows, and that before an amphitheatre was raised the solidity of the foundations should be checked.*

TACITUS *ANNALS* 4.62–63

╬ ╬ ╬

AD 64   Destruction and renewal

Augustus's amphitheatre burned down in the great fire of Rome. There was no immediate replacement as the city was soon afterwards convulsed by civil war. The eventual winner, Vespasian, set about building the ultimate gladiatorial theatre – the Amphitheatrum Flavium, later known as the Colosseum.

OPPOSITE   *Wooden amphitheatre, built by the lowest-bidding contractor. Enter at your own risk.*
RIGHT   *The Flavian Amphitheatre. Stone-built to the highest specifications; 2,000-year guarantee.*

AD 80   The Flavian amphitheatre opens

Spectacular shows were presented by Vespasian's son and successor Titus. The epigrammatist Martial wrote an embarrassingly obsequious description of the games:

╬ ╬ ╬

[In the arena] even warrior Mars serves you, O Caesar, with unconquered arms.

MARTIAL ON *THE SPECTACLES* 8

╬ ╬ ╬

---

* Suetonius says 20,000 died in his *Life of Tiberius*, 40.

AD 107   *Trajan tops them all*

Following his victory in the Dacian wars, Trajan put on games that will probably remain forever unmatched, because never before or since has the empire had such enormous resources at its disposal. In 123 days of games there were animal 'hunts' in which thousands of beasts of all descriptions were slaughtered, and over 5,000 pairs of gladiators fought.

An animal hunt. Skilled venatores, *highly trained to handle and fight savage beasts from all over the empire, bitterly resent being considered a warm-up act for the gladiators.*

Thus we come to the present, when the gladiator, for better or worse, represents Roman culture across the empire, from the Thames to the Tigris. Only the Roman legions have a greater number of men under arms than the gladiator schools of the empire, and every schoolboy knows the name of the top gladiators in his town. As a gladiator you may be a despised outcast, and decent men will turn and hurry their wives aside to avoid meeting you on the street. But you can be sure that the wife will look back over her shoulder as you pass, and later her husband will hurry to the arena to watch you fight. And if he is even half a man, he will wonder what it is like to be there, fighting for his life on the blood-soaked sand.

Codex Gladiorum

Caesar's assassins were protected immediately after the deed by a bodyguard of gladiators supplied by Decimus Brutus.

✣

In Rome, the *aediles* were given public funds to stage games as part of their duties as city magistrates. Many, such as Caesar sought to attract votes for their future career by tacking on extra features such as gladiatorial games at their own expense.

✣

A rare example of gladiators participating in a full-scale war came when Octavian (the future Augustus) was besieging Perusia in Italy. He was nearly trapped by a party of enterprising gladiators who made a sortie from the walls.

✣

Pliny the Elder tells us that because they usually fought at funerals, gladiators were once called *bustuaria*. (*Bustum* means 'cemetery'.)

✣

Thumelicus, the infant son of the German leader Arminius (author of the Teutoberg massacre of the Roman legions in AD 9) was captured by the Romans. Raised in Ravenna, by some reports he was trained to be a gladiator and probably died in the arena.

✣

Gladiators from the region of Dacia are now so common that 'The Dacian' gladiatorial school in Rome is named after them.

- - - - - - - - - - - - - - - - - -

ABOVE *Dacian warriors – coming soon to an arena near you.*

Arenas of the Empire

Do things to prove to yourself who you are, not to impress the world.

HANDBOOK OF EPICTETUS THE STOIC 47

✛ ✛ ✛

M any gladiators live and die without ever seeing the amphitheatre in Rome. (In Rome, the citizens only mean one building when they say 'the amphitheatre'. That's the Amphitheatrum Flavium, the gift of the emperor Vespasian to the people of Rome. We shall come to that amphitheatre in due course.) Rome is an empire as well as a city, and like Rome's baths, aqueducts and laws, the cult of the gladiator has spread far beyond the shores of Italy. So this chapter will show some of the options that exist for the discerning *auctoratus* beyond the meat-factories of the imperial schools in Rome itself. (If you are not an *auctoratus*, of course, you go where you are sent, and will probably die within a short distance of the court that dispatched you to the arena in the first place.)

1 See Ephesus and die

✛ ✛ ✛

If, in the manner of men, I have fought with beasts at Ephesus, what advantage is it to me? If the dead do not rise, 'Let us eat and drink; for tomorrow we die'.

ST PAUL *1 CORINTHIANS* 15.32

✛ ✛ ✛

Pros	Cons
1 Excellent location	1 Unusual opponent types
2 Civilized fans	2 Not a custom-built arena
3 Top-notch health care	3 High-quality opposition

Arrival

How about fighting in the romantic east of the empire, where the Silk Road brings in rare and exotic goods from the other side of the world, and where Aramaic and Greek are heard more often than Latin? Take ship to the eastern shores of the Mediterranean, just past the rock-bound island of Chios, to where the mountains of Samos slip by on the right and the coast of Asia Minor becomes visible in the haze ahead. The rocky ridge of Mount Coressus rears against the skyline, marking a break in the hills several miles wide, and in that break lie sandy beaches, the mouth of the river Cayster, and the harbour of Panormus.

Just beyond the harbour is the bustling city of Ephesus, foremost city of Asia Minor, and – since the time of Hadrian a generation ago – the seat of Rome's provincial government. The Praetorium, Rome's version of Government House, sits prominently on one of the ridges at the foot of Mount Coressus. Let your eye run past the Praetorium to a smaller nearby hill with a double peak shaped like the flattened humps of one of the Bactrian camels which bring spice from the deep hinterland. This hill is called Mount Pion, and there, nestling in the cleft between these two peaks, carved into the hillside, is a huge theatre capable of seating tens of thousands of spectators. That's the arena of Ephesus, where the gladiators fight. Gladiatorial games are well established in Asia Minor, though some affect to despise them as an affront to the Greek humanistic tradition. This attitude is more common among those of the educated upper classes such as the rhetorician Dio Chrysostom (literally, 'he of the golden mouth'), but make no mistake, the theatre is packed for each gladiatorial performance. Even the children sketch graffiti of gladiators in action, and in this they are no different from youngsters all over the empire, who regularly play at 'gladiator'.

✢ ✢ ✢

Like children who play at being wrestlers, then a bit later, at being gladiators, then blowing the trumpets…

EPICTETUS *DISCOURSES* 3.77

✢ ✢ ✢

The first games recorded in Ephesus were staged during the wars against Mithridates in 69 BC, in the time of the Late Republic. So popular were the games that the old theatre was modified to make it suitable for gladiatorial games.

✣ ✣ ✣

Who does not think that gladiator contests and wild beast shows are the most fascinating things?

ATHENAGORAS *EMBASSY FOR THE CHRISTIANS* 35

✣ ✣ ✣

Getting the jargon

Anyone coming from the Latin west has to get used to the fact that gladiators are called athletes. This is just one of several new terms that you will need to learn.

- An eastern amphitheatre is often called a *stadium* (because that's where athletes perform).
- Watch out for an opponent called 'unsurpassed in skill' because the term means he is an undefeated veteran.
- Out here the event in which you fight is called a *philotimia* instead of a *munus*.
- Room-mates at the *ludus* are *synkelarioi*.
- A good fighter ends up with a band of enthusiastic *philoploi*, or fans.
- A bad fighter needs to learn the term *apeluthe*, the Latin *missus*, which means he has been spared.

Looking around

Ephesus is a popular place to live. Every year huge swarms of tourists descend on the city to participate in or watch the Artemisia, the festival of Diana, the maiden goddess whom the Greeks call Artemis. Here, Diana is more than just a goddess of hunting, as she is in Greece and Rome. In Asia she has become conflated with several other goddesses, and is regarded as the patron goddess of the entire province. So fervent is the cult of Diana that when a wandering preacher called Paulus came here to spread his Gospel, the population came so close to lynching him that it inspired the line about being thrown to 'the beasts', which is quoted on p. 40. It may well be that the following line, 'eat and drink; for tomorrow we die' refers to the traditional feast on the eve of the games – the *cena libera* – which is given both to gladiators and the condemned, not only in Ephesus, but in all gladiatorial venues, including Rome.

One of the first things an aspiring Ephesian gladiator should do is make a visit to the great temple of Diana, to seek the blessing and favour of the Maiden. Piety aside, it is certain the locals will approve, and one cannot start collecting a claque of supporters too soon. There are other reasons for going to the temple, one being that the Temple of Diana is one of the seven wonders of the world and well worth seeing for its own sake. The current temple is not the original, which was built with funds from the fabulously wealthy Croesus of Lydia, but an equally awesome replacement. Within is a statue of Diana, which the

The goddess Diana, protector of beast-fighters in arenas throughout the empire. This statue shows her as she appears to her worshippers in the temple in Ephesus.

locals will tell you was set in place by Jupiter himself. The local silver merchants sell small copies, which might make a suitable good-luck charm or mini-shrine back in the *ludus*.

Another reason for a lusty young gladiator to visit the temple is because many of the young ladies who hang around there are, well, considerably less than maidenly, and prepared to demonstrate the fact for a small fee.

The arena

The arena is a very respectable size, some 300 by 160 yards, so there is considerable freedom of manoeuvre. The bad news is that this encourages the more enterprising type of *editor* to consider novelty events, and a gladiator who is used to being matched against standard gladiator types will take a dim view of having to fight horsemen or chariots. They would never do such things in Rome, where a specialist swordsman sits out purely horse-oriented combats such as cavalry v. chariots. Be advised that the Thracian type of gladiator is popular here, as is the *murmillo* (see pp 78–79 for what these types mean). The heavily armed Samnite type is almost unknown, but the region has in the past boasted some especially deadly net-fighters (*retiarii*). There is also a type called the *scissor*, rarely seen outside the east, who exchanges the standard shield for an armoured sleeve (*manica*) with a hook or a strange four-bladed knife fixed to the end.

✝ ✝ ✝

And among the gladiators, I see not just those who are beast-like, but Greeks too...

PLUTARCH *MORALIA* 1099B

✝ ✝ ✝

A murmillo *and a* Thracian *get up close and personal in this bas-relief from Ephesus. Note the wide gladiator's belts, and the viciously-hooked* Thracian *knife at the* murmillo's *back.*

Barely 100 yards from the arena is the gladiator cemetery, where the tiro can wander around picking up handy hints from his predecessors, such as one Pandos. He was a local lad, whose tombstone boasts of his having won ten fights. In one case, though the sun was in his eyes, he slew his opponent 'like a donkey'. Remember that the twin humps of Mount Pion are easily visible from the arena, and keep them in view. If you let yourself be turned too far away from Pion, the afternoon sun over the sea might shine a blinding light into your helmet.

Remember also that this is not a custom-designed arena. The morning fights often feature bulls, which have a lot of blood in them, and drainage is imperfect. Lazy attendants and slippery blood pools under a patch of fresh sand do not a helpful combination make.

Alternative venues

Pergamum Former provincial capital, where the great Galen was gladiator doctor.

Halicarnassus Also does novelty acts such as woman gladiators.

Athens Where gladiator sports have recently become very popular.

✛ ✛ ✛

Crowds of Athenians swarmed to the theatre below the Acropolis to witness the human slaughter.

PHILOSTRATUS *LIFE OF APOLLONIUS OF TYANA* 4.22

✛ ✛ ✛

Chances of survival

Not bad at all. A lot depends on who is the current priest of the imperial cult. He has to pay the *ludus* for every gladiator killed in the arena, and as his job entails many other expenses besides, he is definitely pulling for you to get through alive. The tighter his budget, the more this becomes the case.

Carving of a gladiator from Halicarnassus. Unusually, this figure has no protective padding on the legs or sword-arm – perhaps an aesthetic choice by the sculptor.

- - - - - - - -

A moneybags prepared to buy popularity with the lives of gladiators is the worst possible scenario.

In general health terms Ephesus has plenty of good fresh food from the Meander river valley. The city also sits on the crossroads of the east-west spice road and the north-south trade route that continues south through the Magnesian Gate not far from the arena. So one has plentiful provisions, fresh fish, and a healthy breeze from the sea. Infection and the plague are less of a risk here than in Rome.

Furthermore – apart from the regular risk that lethal amounts of steel might interfere with one's metabolism – gladiators are much better off than the general population. In addition to a good diet and healthy exercise, they have the best medical care available. Galen, one of the greatest doctors of the age, practised his craft on the gladiators of the arena of nearby Pergamum before going on to become the personal physician of the late emperor Marcus Aurelius. (Aurelius passed through Ephesus on his way to campaign in the east – there is still a statue of him and his brother Lucius Verus, and a very young Commodus, which commemorates the event.)

Finally, Ephesus has a host of other games such as the Ephasia, the Olympia and the Adriana. These are contests of athletics in the non-gladiatorial sense, and competitions of music, poetry and drama, in which people are only cut dead at the social events after the games. (There are plenty of these – the procession of the maidens at the Artemisia is so splendid that it was immortalized by the famous painter Apelles, and many a young man or maid comes to the Artemisia for the specific purpose of finding a spouse.)

All this jollity means less time available on the calendar for gladiatorial games, so with luck the city will only set aside one or two occasions per year for killing time. That's not to say a tiro's chances are good, especially in the first year, but things get better after that, and if you have to go, Ephesus is not a bad departure point.

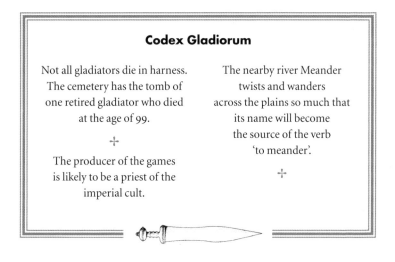

Codex Gladiorum

Not all gladiators die in harness. The cemetery has the tomb of one retired gladiator who died at the age of 99.

✛

The producer of the games is likely to be a priest of the imperial cult.

The nearby river Meander twists and wanders across the plains so much that its name will become the source of the verb 'to meander'.

✛

2 See Carthage and die

Pros	Cons
1 Good arena	1 Telegenic types stealing the limelight
2 Lively circus	
3 Luxurious baths	2 Too many Christians to kill
4 Good theatre	3 It gets very hot in a helmet
	4 Demanding audience

Any Roman making port in Carthage's famous circular harbour cannot help remembering that it was from here that the great fleets of Carthage sailed against Rome, and from here that Hannibal took ship to Spain, from there to invade Italy over the Alps with elephants also probably shipped from this very spot. Of course, these days the inhabitants will assure you that they are solid Roman citizens, and in no way related to the baby-burning barbaric Phoenicians who once occupied the site. Carthage is now a Roman colony, and many inhabitants are the descendants of retired Augustan legionaries. There is also a large Punic quarter, but these people too have a truly Roman appreciation of lethal arena sports.

Looking around

In fact the Carthaginians, both Roman and native, do not stint themselves for entertainment. Just to the south of the amphitheatre is a huge circus for chariot racing, which is only 100 yards shorter than the Circus Maximus in Rome itself. To the north is a well-appointed theatre, and the city has splendid baths built a few decades ago with marble floors and elegant columns of onyx and porphyry. Alas, these baths are on the opposite side of town to the amphitheatre, so getting there is no trivial task. (The walls of Carthage are 23 miles long.)

The amphitheatre

Carthage is the capital of Roman Africa, and predictably it has an amphitheatre to match its status. The building is just three quarters of a mile from the core of the city, which is centred on the forum on Brysa Hill.

Downhill and to the west of the forum is the arena. It is a standard oval shape of respectable size (175 by 140 yards), or about the same size as the amphitheatre in Pompeii. Carthage's arena was rebuilt with limestone in AD 165 after a fire devastated much of the city, and no expense has been spared. For example, there are bronze crampons to hold the stone blocks together, each crampon sheathed in lead to protect it from the elements.

Within, the audience can expect to be musically entertained by a hydraulic organ, while they admire the magnificent statues placed around the arena. The goddess Caelestis seated on a lion is a popular motif here, as Caelestis is the patron of the city, the old Punic moon-goddess Tanit, in a thin Roman disguise.

There is an underground vault so that animals and prisoners can be introduced directly into the arena, but the beasts are generally kept in cages at ground level around the sides, so that some front-row seats are actually over the creatures. The wall around the arena itself is low enough to require a defensive net, which prevents athletic leopards from becoming personally acquainted with the spectators. Seating capacity is relatively limited, but only from the point of view of those who feel 15,000 is too small an audience.

The Carthaginians take their gladiator combats very seriously, and anyone who has a modest success soon starts finding little curse tablets turning up with his name on them. These curses are from unsuccessful gamblers who buy little lead jinxes damning the gladiator they bet against to the infernal gods of the underworld.

Alternative venues

There is talk of an even larger and more spectacular amphitheatre being built down the road at Thysdrus, a city where you can hardly move for jumped-up entrepreneurs who made millions in the olive-oil export business.

Bless the beasts

The fly in the gladiatorial ointment in these parts is the damnable guild of the Telegenii. Because Africa is abundantly stocked with a huge variety of wild animals with great potential for entertainment, beast-hunters almost upstage gladiators in the popular imagination. The best-known guild of *venatores*, as beast-fighters are known, is the Telegenii. Their distinctive

Animal fighters upstage their gladiator colleagues in this mosaic from North Africa. Venatores sometimes fight in pairs, so that one can distract the beast from a hard-pressed team-mate.

symbol is a crescent-bladed spear – a not-so-subtle reference to the crescent moon of Tanit, who is still respected by the large native population in most audiences. However, the 'official' patron of the guild is Bacchus, and it is a testament to the popularity of the guild that Bacchus's statue has a prominent place in the Carthaginian arena.

Bacchus, patron god of wine and the Telegenii. It is perhaps appropriate that the Telegenii have chosen a god whose worshippers have been known to rip apart innocent bystanders in a bestial frenzy.

The two consolations for a gladiator are, first, that the Telegenii are a touring troupe, who do shows in all the North African venues, and so are out of town for prolonged periods. Secondly, the beast-fighters do not always get things their own way, as this clumsy attempt to execute two Christian martyrs in the arena of Carthage demonstrates.

✝ ✝ ✝

*To start with, he [the martyr Saturus] and Revocatus were put against a
leopard, and then while in the stocks they were attacked by a bear. Saturus
dreaded bears above all, and he intended to be killed by one bite of a leopard.
But he was to be paired with a wild boar. In fact, the venator who was tying
him to the animal got gored by the boar and died a few days afterwards,
whereas Saturus was only dragged along. Then when he was tied up waiting
for the bear, the animal refused to come out of its cage.*

THE PASSION OF ST PERPETUA 19

✝ ✝ ✝

*An animal hunt in full swing. A bull and a bear are literally joined in combat,
and an unfortunate prisoner is given the task of separating them. Another
participant is punished for his understandable unenthusiasm.*

A leopard dying in the arena costs the organizer 1,000 or 2,000 *sestertii*. This
is cheaper than a gladiator, but – like a gladiator – a well-known leopard
might be spared for another day. The fact that animals in Africa are relatively inexpensive explains why the editor will put on beast-shows rather
than gladiator fights as often as the crowd will permit, and the Carthaginian
crowd permits it a lot.

Chances of survival

Even if there is a chance of being upstaged by the *venatores* in the morning,
expect to have to perform in the afternoon, and perform relatively often. As
Carthage is the provincial capital, the high priest of the imperial cult is the

sacerdos provinciae Africae – the high priest of the whole province – and he is expected to stage appropriately lavish games. Lesser games are staged, for example, by local officials to celebrate their election.

✜ ✜ ✜

At the gladiator's midday show we laughed at Mercury testing the dead with a red hot iron [to make sure they were really dead]... and watched the taking away of the corpses of the gladiators.

TERTULLIAN *APOLOGIA* 15.5

✜ ✜ ✜

An unpleasant aspect of the job is that gladiators might be called on to execute prisoners in the arena, a task that bestows neither dignity nor honour. Christianity is growing in popularity and bringing a steady flow of martyrs of all ages and classes. The crowd will call on gladiators to finish off any who survive the beasts, and even a gladiator who has no hesitation in killing in the heat of a fight may well hesitate before plunging his sword into the throat of a defenceless young woman.

✜ ✜ ✜

Perpetua, however, had yet to taste more pain. She screamed as she was struck in the ribs; then she took the wavering hand of the young gladiator and guided it to her throat.

THE PASSION OF ST PERPETUA 21

✜ ✜ ✜

By reputation the Punic people are famously cruel, and even native Romans are less inclined to mercy than their contemporaries in the Greek east, so it is a good idea to try to make sure that it is your opponent who has to plead for the mercy of the crowd. And if your appeal fails, well, there are worse places to spend eternity than the necropolis in Carthage. It's in a beautiful location, which looks across the bay to where the Mediterranean blends into the darker blue of the mountains on the horizon.

Codex Gladiorum

In the AD 130s Quintus Voltedius Optatus gave four days of gladiatorial combats and beast fights in Carthage at a cost of 200,000 *sestertii*. (A workman might get 500 *sestertii* in a year.)

✠

Not just the *venatores*, but also some individual leopards are known to the crowd by name.

✠

Arena themes are popular in local mosaics, so there's a chance of being immortalized in stone tesserae.

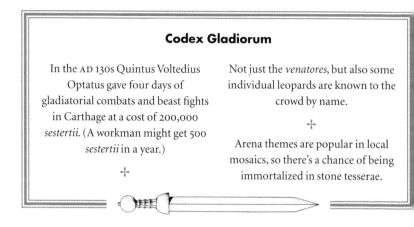

3 See Londinium and die

✠ ✠ ✠

[For] Beryllus, a Greek essedarius [chariot fighter] aged 25, freed after his 20th combat. His wife Nomas set up this for her well-deserving husband.

MEMORIAL FOR A GLADIATOR *CIL* 12.3323

✠ ✠ ✠

Pros	Cons
1 Good fighting surface	1 Still the edge of the world
2 The sun seldom blinds you	2 If your opponents don't get you, lumbago might
3 Improving facilities	3 Lots of competition for your place

When he thinks of it at all, which is not often, the average Roman still pictures Britannia as a foggy island on the edge of the world filled with feral bears and Britons. About the only Briton most Romans can name is Boudicca, and she is hardly a fond memory. Yet this view does a considerable injustice to an island that is rapidly developing into one of the empire's most prosperous provinces.

Looking around

On arriving at what the natives used to call Llyn Din (the 'fortress on the lake'), it's not hard to see signs of growing prosperity, from the number of merchant ships at the docks to the stone houses where tile has replaced thatch on most rooftops. There's a large and generously appointed wall which lets one know that Boudicca has not been forgotten in these parts either. After all, she did raze Londinium to the ground, and even today the only bridge over the Thames is wooden, making it easy to demolish in the face of an advancing army. (Although, with the south peaceful for well over a century now, the main hazard is for the British fishermen who shoot the rapids of the bridge's pilings in their tiny coracles.)

✢ ✢ ✢

London, a city…of busy merchants and abundant provisions.

TACITUS *ANNALS* 14.33

✢ ✢ ✢

The arena

This lies on the east side of the city where a small stream provides water and takes away waste from the minor fort nearby, where the local garrison can be expected to take a professional interest in proceedings. The same stream has made the area just beyond the amphitheatre into a boggy rubbish-tip.

Like many Roman amphitheatres, this one is aligned on an east-west axis, allowing the big-wigs in the *tribunalia* (boxes) the benefit of the sun as they sit on the north side with a view across the shortest part of the oval arena. (Though note that the British weather makes being blinded by the sun or stifled by the heat less of a hazard than in, say, Carthage.)

The old wooden amphitheatre has been replaced by a more substantial edifice, which has brickwork layered with native stone. Because the arena is on a slope, the seats on one side are actually built into the bank. There's a splendidly wide entrance tunnel to the arena, partly to accommodate *Ursus arctos*, the British brown bear. The bears are led in through here and caged in rooms just off the arena entrance, where they fight the same captured Britons from the north that the gladiators occasionally have to face.

(Britons and brown bears are equally ferocious and shaggy, the main difference being that the Britons are dyed blue.) There are no trapdoors in this arena, because just keeping the surface above the local water-table is enough of a problem, let alone excavations below it.

That said, the arena itself is a pleasant enough fighting ground, about 70 yards across at its widest point, and more open on the downhill side. This makes it a very respectable arena as these things go in the western empire, but not comparable to some of the epic structures elsewhere.

The competition

One of the problems facing a British gladiator is that the province is still an active war zone. This not only means that a constant stream of arena-fodder arrives from the north, but you get discharged legionaries down on their luck signing up with the *ludi* as well. Add novelty acts such as woman gladiators (see pp 113–116) and it is harder for an aspiring gladiator to make a name for himself here than in more settled areas.

Mosaic from Britain showing a retiarius *and a* secutor *in combat. Note the lavish decoration on the* secutor's *shield, and the trapdoor which the* retiarius *is hoping he will trip over.*

✛ ✛ ✛

A gladiator considers it demeaning to be matched against an inferior opponent. He knows there is no glory in a victory without danger.

SENECA *ON PROVIDENCE* 3.4

✛ ✛ ✛

This exquisite vase from Colchester shows the retiarius *Valentinus, bereft of net and trident, surrendering to give the* secutor *Memnon his ninth victory.*

Britons might fight as Galli, a type of arena warrior extinct elsewhere in the empire, where the more common Thracian type has replaced them. However, the weapons and tactics of the Britons are very suited to this gladiator type, so it is no surprise that it has survived here. There is, of course, the ubiquitous net-fighter, the *retiarius*, and his traditional opponents the *murmillo* and *secutor*. Many an ex-legionary chooses to fight as a Samnite or *provocator*, since the armour and weapons are compatible with legionary training. (See pp 77–79 for an explanation of these types.) However, Britain is becoming known as a gladiator venue, and professionals from as far afield as Halicarnassus in Asia Minor have been known to come over and try their luck here.

Alternative venues

The presence of the army means that there are opportunities in the provinces for those who can't hack it in the big city:

Chester Has a large amphitheatre, centrally located.

Caerleon Here, the audience is mostly legionaries.

Durnovaria The largest ampitheatre in Britain, made from a converted Neolithic stone circle built two millennia earlier.

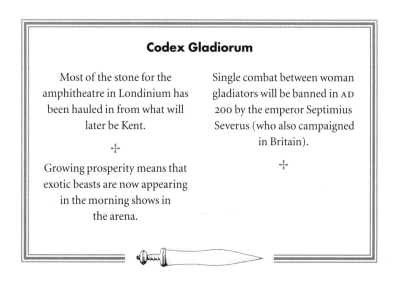

Codex Gladiorum

Most of the stone for the amphitheatre in Londinium has been hauled in from what will later be Kent.

✛

Growing prosperity means that exotic beasts are now appearing in the morning shows in the arena.

Single combat between woman gladiators will be banned in AD 200 by the emperor Septimius Severus (who also campaigned in Britain).

✛

✥ IV ✥
Ludus Life

You are an actor in a drama…you do not choose your part,
but you can choose to play it well.

HANDBOOK OF EPICTETUS THE STOIC 17

✥ ✥ ✥

To enter a *ludus*, or gladiator school, is to become part of another world. Things are different here. There is another set of values, conversation is larded with incomprehensible jargon and life follows a different rhythm. Manners, dress and diet are completely changed, and there is a new set of social relationships, which the tiro must grasp immediately if he is to find his place in this tightly knit community. Above all, within the *ludus* there is a sense that the universe consists of 'us', the people of the amphitheatre, and 'them', which is basically the rest of the world, but especially those who pay for or attend the spectacles.

In many ways the *ludus* is like a large family, and indeed some schools are referred to as *familia gladiatoria* (though anyone considering the gladiators a band of brothers should be prepared for some pretty deadly sibling rivalry). And if the *ludus* is a family, the undoubted patriarch, godfather, and undisputed master is the *lanista*.

✥ ✥ ✥

The familia set this up in memory of [the late] Saturnilos.

ROMAN INSCRIPTION IN LGOG 241

✥ ✥ ✥

The *lanista*

✛ ✛ ✛

He was skilful in every technique of cruelty, battening his profits
with tortures and executions, just as a lanista does in the games.

AMMIANUS MARCELLINUS *HISTORY* 18.12.1

✛ ✛ ✛

In the outside world, the *lanista* is so despised that the priests who pay for many of the spectacles will try to avoid contamination by dealing with him through an intermediary. The trade of the *lanista* is as old as that of the gladiator, and in fact many Romans believe the word, like the gladiator himself, is of Etruscan origin. They point to the Etruscan root of the Latin word *laniare*, which means to 'cut or mutilate'; which is why to the Romans a *lanius* is a butcher. But however contemptible he may seem to those outside his world (and many respectable cemeteries won't even accept his corpse), within the gladiator school the *lanista* is lord of all he surveys.

It is the *lanista* who decides whether to bring on youngsters with potential within the school or to buy in existing talent from outside. He sets the training regime, and keeps a close eye on the budget. He can fine, flog or even execute all in his power, and that includes the *auctorati* who have submitted to him voluntarily. He is the last man a trainee gladiator wants to offend, because he will be literally the last man the trainee offends (before his career is cut short – along with the rest of him – by, for example, an unfortunate pairing against Brutus Britannicus Thrax, the Baby-Eating Barbarian of Britain).

The regime of a *lanista* sets the tone for life in the school. It was the extreme brutality of life in his *ludus* that caused Spartacus and his fellow gladiators to make their famous break for freedom. Some *lanistae* may believe that turning gladiators into savage beasts gets the best results, but the better sort will concentrate on building an esprit de corps and giving gladiators pride in themselves and their profession.

✛ ✛ ✛

*Through no misconduct of theirs, but through the tyranny
of their lanista, they were kept in close confinement apart
from gladiatorial combats.*

PLUTARCH *LIFE OF CRASSUS* 8

✛ ✛ ✛

In the imperial schools, the *lanista* is 'overseen' by a *procurator*, but this official is probably a placeman given his berth as part of the Roman system of swapping favours – including jobs – among the elite. A *procurator* is unlikely to care about the day-to-day running of the place, so long as the gladiators make him look good by their performance when they eventually reach the arena. In smaller or private schools the *procurator* is replaced by a member of the local city council or by the owner of the school itself. For a trainee gladiator, in a large *ludus* contact with such authority figures is rare – the imperial *ludi* in Rome have hundreds of gladiators in their number, few of whom ever have to interact with imperial officials. In fact, one role of the *lanista* is to be an intermediary between the upper management and the gladiators.

Permanent staff

By the nature of their job, gladiators are temporary members of a *ludus*. Most relationships between gladiators and permanent staff are short-lived, basically because most gladiators are short-lived as well. Nevertheless, starting on the right foot with the permanent staff is an essential step for any novice gladiator who plans to leave the school alive.

First aid

One important member of staff, from your point of view, is the *medicus*. Generally speaking, even the smallest gladiator school will have a medic in constant attendance, or at least on retainer, because although gladiatorial combats are relatively rare, injuries in training are commonplace, and the heavy wooden training sword is more than capable of snapping bone. Furthermore, gladiators are as subject to illness as the rest of the population, and every *lanista*'s nightmare is a bout of infectious illness sweeping through the gladiator barracks on the eve of a big show. It is the *medicus* who decides how much tender loving care an injured gladiator receives, and who arranges some rudimentary physiotherapy to ensure, for example, that scar tissue does not affect mobility.

Running repairs. From time immemorial, wherever there have been fighters, there have been medics standing by to patch them up afterwards. As this engraving indicates, many of the best medical practitioners in Rome are Greeks.

Coaching

The *medicus* is not to be confused with the *doctor*. The *doctor* is so called because he has a Ph.D (Potential for huge Damage) in his particular fighting speciality, and it is his task to impart that potential to his trainees. He is expert in the armour, use of weapons, and tactics of the trainee's selected discipline. Almost certainly, he will have extensive experience of using those arms and tactics in the only conditions that count – fighting in the arena. The *doctor* will act as a coach, and depending on the size of the establishment he will double as, or work closely with, the *magister*, who is a more general trainer and keeps an eye on the overall fitness and diet of those in the school.

Armour

The imperial *ludi* have (of course) the most extensive support infrastructure, but the same pattern is mirrored to some extent in every gladiatorial school. Probably only an imperial *ludus* would have a *manicarius* (grade II) for the repair of the padded arm guards many gladiators wear in combat, but even the most down-market gladiator school needs someone to knock missing rivets back into armour, or convert a standard bit of second-hand military kit into something that looks flashy and glamorous (at least from a short distance).

Items of gladiator display armour. A tiro can't expect to wear anything like this for at least six months. His training kit is cruder – and heavier.

Costume

Nor should one underestimate the *vestarius*, who prepares the rest of a gladiator's costume. This role is more important than it seems. Not only does this individual ensure that you are literally dressed to kill, but how a fighter looks is second only to how he behaves when it comes to attracting a following in the crowd. And it may be the crowd who decides whether a defeated gladiator lives or dies.

The back office

As well as those who work directly with the gladiators there are others, equally essential to the life of the *ludus*, but with whom the gladiator rarely interacts. Among these are the clerks who balance the costs of feeding, training and equipment for the gladiators with the payments for their appearances in shows. They say every man has his price, and these clerks know yours down to the last *sestertius*.

Servi

Finally there are the slaves. These perform the background tasks of cleaning, cooking, bringing water and maintaining the latrines. Their basic role is to ensure that a trainee gladiator need do nothing but concentrate on his sole purpose in life – learning how to kill people as stylishly as possible. The very nature of their job encourages some gladiators to be brutal towards the slaves, but this is one area where a bit of kindness can pay dividends. Slaves get everywhere and, because they are generally ignored, they can pick up vital scraps of information, such as advance notice of who might be paired with whom in the coming bouts.

Like a slave owner, a lanista *has the right to chastise those under his tutelage in any way he sees fit. The twisted cords of the* flagellum, *used here, are believed to inflict more pain than a standard short whip.*

The pecking / stabbing order

Conditions within the *ludus* vary greatly according to the status of the gladiator. The different disciplines are usually quartered separately, so that for example, the chasers (*secutores*, p. 78) don't mingle much with the net-men (*retiarii*, p. 79). A cunning *lanista* will play the different groups off against each other, so there is a genuine rivalry between the factions. This adds a bit of extra spice when their representatives meet in the arena.

✛ ✛ ✛

At least a lanista runs a decent establishment. The wimpish skirmisher (psilus) and the well-armoured heavy (euhoplo) are kept well away from each other. A net-man doesn't have to share meals with convicted felons, so that in the room where he strips off to fight no one's going to steal his shoulder guard and trident. Even the dregs of the arena live separately.

JUVENAL *SATIRES* 6

Gladiators have thoroughly infected the popular imagination – spin-off products, such as this oil lamp, find eager buyers all over the empire.

Ideally each class of gladiators in a school should have their own quarters. Again, the paragon is the imperial model, where the gladiators are not only kept separate, but live in their separate *ludi* – one each for the most popular types. Still, in the highly structured world of the gladiator school not even those sharing a barrack room are equals.

✛ ✛ ✛

Lucius Asicius...muriola es!

(THIS INSCRIPTION BY JESUS, A RIVAL IN POMPEII, INFORMS LUCIUS
ASICIUS – A *MURMILLO* OR 'FISH MAN' TYPE GLADIATOR – THAT HE
IS EITHER A STINKY FISH PASTE OR A DRINK FAVOURED BY WOMEN,
DEPENDING WHICH TRANSLATION ONE PREFERS)

✛ ✛ ✛

The rough hierarchy in a group of gladiators is as follows.

The primus palus

The name reflects the Roman love of puns, this one being on the *primus pilus*, the leading centurion in a legion. The *palus* in question is the training post, with which a rookie will soon become intimately familiar.

Often the *primus palus* is a gladiator who has signed on again after serving out his original contract. A skilled veteran fighter, he may also serve as the *doctor* who coaches others.

The secundus palus

The *primus palus* also fights in the arena (and when he is paired with his opposite number in another discipline, expect the stands to be packed with spectators). Therefore, most schools have a *secundus palus*, who is ready to step into the sandals of a deceased *primus* at short notice.

These top fighters in a school are volunteers, and may even go home to their wives and children at the end of the day. Even so, each still comes back in the morning and spends hours training as though his life depended on it. Because it does.

✢ ✢ ✢

Eorta and Asklepiades set up this memorial for Danoas, their husband and father. He was second palus of the Thracians [a gladiator type, p. 79] and after nine combats, he departed to the afterlife.

MEMORIAL FOR A GLADIATOR FROM
CYZICUS IN ASIA MINOR. LGOG 293

✢ ✢ ✢

After surviving several fights, a gladiator might well have enough savings for a funeral monument. This fighter obviously left his family in comfortable circumstances.

Veteres

These are gladiators who have survived at least one bout in the arena. There is a distinction between those who fought and won and those who fought and lost, but obtained a *missio* – i.e. were spared death after defeat. Remember that most *missiones* come as the reward for a very well-fought bout, so this category of veteran is not to be despised.

It is less common for fighters in the top two ranks to be *damnati ad gladium* – those sentenced to die by the sword, who will never leave the *ludus* alive. However, there are plenty of *damnati* among the veterans. Such gladiators often win, because they fight like men who literally have nothing to lose.

✜ ✜ ✜

*Gladiators…fear fighting no adversary more than one who has
no chance of life, but who can still kill…a man who has no expectation
of the missio will attack naked the same opponent he would
otherwise flee from even if armed.*

SENECA *CONTROVERSIES* 9.6

✜ ✜ ✜

The veterans of the arena have their own grading system, and it is one of which they are intensely proud. That is their count of appearances and victories. A man who has fought six times and won five, for example, counts himself superior to a man who has won two of his four bouts – although the quality of the opposition is also taken into account. A gladiator with a good number of victories will try to have the fact emblazoned on his tombstone.

This aspect of the gladiatorial scoring system has been taken up enthusiastically by the wider community. Before every appearance of gladiators in the arena, posters advertise who will compete and the number of their previous appearances and victories. Betting on gladiator fights is frowned upon by the authorities, but a gladiator's previous form is one of the major factors that influence the odds in the betting on his survival or victory.

✣ ✣ ✣

Maximus, essedarius [a gladiator who fights from a chariot, p. 80]
from the Ludus Juliani. 40 combats, 36 victories.

VETERAN GLADIATOR'S SCORECARD ON A
ROMAN INSCRIPTION. *CIL* 6.33952

✣ ✣ ✣

Tirones

These are the virgin gladiators, men under arms who have never yet had to fight for their lives in the arena. Even among these beginners there are distinctions.

At the top of the tiro tree are the *auctorati*, those who came into the school of their own volition – however little choice circumstance actually allowed them.

Then there are the *damnati* – who are themselves divided into the *damnati ad gladium* and the *damnati ad ludos*, since the latter have a chance of redemption (pp 9–10). The *auctorati* will only see these groups at training, since they are true prisoners of the school – confined to barracks, or even locked in their cells at night.

Yet those *damnati* who will fight as individuals can still find someone else to look down on, namely the *gregarii*, those gladiators of so little value that they fight against each other in packs. The *gregarii* will in turn differentiate themselves into 'civilized men' and barbarians (the latter being probably prisoners of war).

Since even his adoring fans consider a *primus palus* beneath contempt, it is hard to imagine what a barbarian *gregarius* looks down on. Socially speaking, this is truly rock bottom. Yet even here, as the Stoic philosopher Seneca points out, valour in death can bring a degree of redemption and respect.

✣ ✣ ✣

One of the barbarians sank into his own throat a spear with which he was armed
against his foes. 'Why should I be armed and still wait for death and
humiliation?' he asked…And from this we learn that it can be more honourable
to die than to kill.

SENECA *LETTERS* 7.26

✣ ✣ ✣

Of another barbarian fighter who committed suicide, Seneca comments in the same letter:

✛ ✛ ✛

We need not imagine only great men have the fortitude to break free from the chains of slavery. …Certainly this brave fellow was entitled to choose his death, but how gallantly he would have wielded a sword!

SENECA *LETTERS* 7.20 FF

✛ ✛ ✛

Diet

The motto of gladiator cookery is quantity over quality. Gladiators in training shovel an amazing amount of food through their systems. A lot of this gets burned off or turned into muscle, because, as newcomers are about to discover, there is no training regimen quite as strenuous as that which awaits them. 'They exercise until they drop from fatigue, and then they eat to excess, prolonging their dinners until after midnight,' remarks Galen, who has tended to a gladiator or two in his time.

✛ ✛ ✛

The gladiators are being prepared for a spectacle, so that their blood can sate the lust for cruelty of the onlookers. Their bodies are pumped up with stronger food, and the limbs are fortified with extra muscle and sinew – all so the man being fattened for the slaughter might die a harder death...

CYPRIAN *LETTER TO DONATUS* 7

✛ ✛ ✛

Some of the food gets turned into fat, which is no bad thing. An extra layer of fat acts as a cushion against bruising impacts, and increases the distance a blade has to go before it penetrates something vital. As well as shielding essential nerves and blood vessels, fatty tissue bleeds spectacularly when cut without affecting overall performance greatly. Thus an injured fighter can impress the audience by the heroism with which he battles on though bleeding like a stuck pig.

It's a rare combat that lasts more than a half-hour – in fact, some can be less than a minute – so carrying the extra weight is not an issue (though eventual enfeeblement through blood loss certainly is). Nor do the Romans believe that being overweight is particularly unhealthy, and gladiators anyway face more urgent threats to their life expectancy.

Meat

Despite the vast amount of meat left over from the morning animal hunts, a gladiator's diet is mainly vegetarian. This is because animal hunts, like gladiator fights, are relatively infrequent events, but gladiators eat and train all year round. However, when a gladiator does get to eat meat, this might include tiger steak and elephant-liver fricassee.

✛ ✛ ✛

[They – not just gladiators but some of the general public] dine on the flesh of animals from the arena…though that boar has just been wiped clean of the human blood he spilled, and that stag has wallowed in the blood of a gladiator. They seek the very stomachs of the bears while they are still warm with undigested human flesh.

TERTULLIAN *APOLOGIA* 9.11

✛ ✛ ✛

Barley

One of the main ingredients of the diet is barley, a none-too-subtle reminder of the gladiator's status, since outside the *ludus* this grain is mainly fed to animals. Barley is nutritious, but its side effects include energetic bowel movements and flatulence, which adds a certain piquancy to the atmosphere of a gladiator barrack room on a winter's night.

✛ ✛ ✛

Barley is amongst the oldest of human foods, and this is also shown by gladiators who, from their diet, were once called hordearii [barley-men].

PLINY THE ELDER *NATURAL HISTORY* 18.14

✛ ✛ ✛

Fruit and vegetables

Trainers are fully aware of the importance of a healthy diet for their charges, and while they might not know what vitamins are, they know that their gladiators do not perform well unless they get them. So expect vegetables on the menu, lots of them, and all as fresh as possible.

Bone ash and charred wood

Ash? Indeed. A diet high in carbohydrates and vegetables is low in calcium, and the *ludus* prefers fighters with sturdy bones that bend rather than snap. So the gladiators in training are fed a special brew that pushes their body calcium to levels that later archaeologists will call 'exorbitant'.

So in a world where many people, even some free citizens outside the *ludus*, are dying of cold, malnutrition and lack of basic medical assistance, the gladiator-in-training has warm, secure quarters, medical care fit for an emperor (remember that Galen went on to become physician to Marcus Aurelius) and all the food he can eat. Yes, he has had to sell his body and soul to get it, but some consider the price to be worthwhile.

Training

✛ ✛ ✛

Give yourself up to your trainer as a patient does to his doctor. You may be thrown into a trench [as a corpse], or dislocate your shoulder, wrench an ankle, get stripes whipped across your back and eat dust by the bucket load.

EPICTETUS *DISCOURSES* 3.15

✛ ✛ ✛

There's a reason why gladiators are Rome's premier bodyguards, debt-collectors and enforcers. Simply it's because no one, but no one, can fight like a gladiator. The legions have some formidable fighters in their number, but these men are trained as part of a unit, and have other skills equally valued by their generals, such as the ability to march long distances while carrying heavy loads. When it comes to individual mayhem on a one-to-one basis, the gladiator is basically unbeatable – except by another gladiator.

Bird's-eye view of the Ludus Magnus, with the Flavian Amphitheatre (Colosseum) in the background. Note the training posts set up at one end of the arena. Roofing work in progress allows a view into some rooms. The steps from the entrance lead to the Via Labicana outside.

The reason for this lies in the training, which is long, hard and brutal. Before it begins, the *magister* might announce with relish that he expects a certain percentage of fatalities among his novices, and that he has not reached his quota yet. Instructors in similar circumstances have used such rhetoric from time immemorial, but here in the *ludus* it may be literally true. After all, the death of a gladiator in training is not going to raise any eyebrows in the wider world.

Stage 1

When he first comes to the school, the novice is evaluated by skilled assessors. It is vital to make a good impression here. Weaklings, either physical or mental, have no place in a gladiator school and staff will not waste time, food and expertise on someone who can't stay the course. At worst, someone deemed otherwise useless might be paired against a promising gladiator in the arena. That's training for the lad with potential – so that he gets used to lethal combat and learns to make his first kill.

Stage 2

This is the *palus* mentioned above – basically a wooden post stuck in the ground, at which a gladiator hacks for hour after hour. He wears a helmet and carries a shield heavier than the standard type, and his sword, though wooden, is carefully weighted so that it weighs twice as much as a normal sword.

✛ ✛ ✛

The use of the palus is invaluable in training both soldiers and gladiators. Neither the arena nor the battlefield has seen an unbeaten victor in armed combat who was not first thoroughly trained in this way.

VEGETIUS *MILITARY MATTERS* 1.11

✛ ✛ ✛

Perhaps oddly, given that gladiators live and die by the sword, access to actual cutting weapons is tightly restricted. Swords and suchlike are kept under lock and key, and not just because the authorities remember what happened when Spartacus and his crew got their hands on proper weaponry. Gladiators, especially the *damnati*, are not the most stable of individuals, and the fistfights, general initiations and bullying in the barracks don't bear thinking about should sharp implements get thrown into the mix. The second stage of training has three basic purposes:

1 To teach the basic cuts and blocks every gladiator needs The human body has certain vulnerable points, and limited physical means of striking those points with a sword. Every attack has a defence, and offers potential for a counter-attack. Knowledge and smooth deployment of fighting techniques must become second nature.

✛ ✛ ✛

We can see that every move of a gladiator, either in a defensive parry or in a vigorous attack, is endowed with a kind of graceful fluidity, so that what is useful in combat also becomes attractive to behold.

CICERO *ON THE ORATOR* 228

✛ ✛ ✛

2 To build muscle As any Roman female is aware, gladiators are intensely physical creatures. Brute strength is a prized attribute. The average gladiator is several times stronger than a normal Roman simply because he does nothing but build muscle for hours on end every day while a normal Roman is making a living.

✣ ✣ ✣

After falling into the hands of a lanista, many with well-proportioned bodies become the opposite – hideously distorted creatures overloaded with flesh and blood after their muscles have been developed beyond measure.

GALEN *THE STUDY OF THE ARTS* 4

✣ ✣ ✣

RIGHT *Ornamental statuette of a gladiator wearing a fantastical helmet. So as to make this little decoration more stable, the sculptor has increased the 'padding' on the left leg to a wholly unrealistic degree.*

As Galen well knows (and future excavations of gladiator graveyards will confirm), gladiator bodies are over-muscled to the point of deformity. This puts huge strains on joints and tendons, which will cause numerous physical complications in later life – a hazard that the gladiator gladly accepts in exchange for the prospect of actually having a later life.

3 Assessment for specialized training Up to this point the gladiator's training has been unspecialized. Indeed, recruits to the legions undergo a similar course of weapons training. However, after the tiro has been working at the post for a period (which may last for several months), the *magister* will make an assessment as to the speciality to which he is best suited. In some schools, the tiro may be destined for a particular role – for example a particularly adept senior Thracian-style gladiator might get

through a lot of his Samnite opponents, so a supply of Samnite recruits must be kept on tap.

In the better type of school, the tiro may be tried out in bouts against members of the various disciplines before being allocated to a particular *doctor* to become expert at a specific means of killing. It is at this point that a gladiator's career may be said to have truly begun.

RIGHT *He who lives by the sword ends up on the sword. This Thracian gladiator, carved in bone, forms the handle for a blade.*

Codex Gladiorum

A private troupe of gladiators is generally referred to by the name of the owner. So, for example, Varro's gladiators will be the *familia gladiatoria Varronis*.

✛

Equestrians were the second highest class in Roman society, yet it required a law in 122 BC to prevent them from hiring themselves to *ludi* as gladiators.

✛

A gladiator in Pompeii called himself Telephus after a legendary son of Hercules. As he survived to become a doctor at the *ludus*, perhaps his *nom d'arena* was well chosen.

✛

A good school will have a masseur or two to ease away the pain of post-training aches and bruises.

✛

This dedication describes a munus *featuring a hunt (*venatio*), athletics and gifts (*sparsiones*) and announces awnings to shade the audience from the sun (*vela*). Locals might add their own pictorial contributions to such announcements.*

The Making of a Gladiator

Decide what kind of man you want to be, and be him.

HANDBOOK OF EPICTETUS THE STOIC 33

✤ ✤ ✤

The tiro faces two life-changing choices, which will literally define his identity for the remaining years of service. From the very beginning it will have been made plain that, while ancient, his profession is not an honourable one. Therefore he should follow the example of the even older and equally dishonourable profession of the prostitutes (who do a roaring trade outside the amphitheatre when the gladiators have finished their bouts), and do his dirty work under the cover of an assumed nom de guerre.

This hankering for anonymity is also one reason why some gladiatorial helmets do as good a job of protecting the gladiator's identity as they do of protecting his skull. Nemo the *secutor* can appear in the arena with even his nearest and dearest watching from the stands unaware of his original identity as Marcus Ovis Nero Familiae.*

Spectators sometimes accuse a poorly performing gladiator of being a runaway slave, since slaves are notoriously lacking in moral fibre. An undiscriminating *ludus* does indeed make a secure hideout for those prepared to leap from the frying pan of slavery to the fire of the arena, since, even during his public performances, the identity of the runaway is protected.

Therefore, for a variety of reasons, gladiators assume a variety of names – or have names chosen for them. A gladiator is essentially in show business, and the *lanista* might fancy his marketing skills. Gladiatorial anonymity means that we have no idea who the most famous gladiator in history actually was, since Spartacus adopted the name of a town in Thracia.

---

* The black sheep of the family.

Heroic, ironic, bombastic or iconic?

Names can come from many sources. Mythology offers a rich vein, if one fancies fighting as a Hector or an Ajax (and though calling oneself after the famously invulnerable Achilles might be tempting fate, some gladiators are prepared to take the risk). One gladiator in the past called himself Hermes, the god who leads souls to the underworld. His divine namesake must have approved, for Hermes was indeed highly successful. The poet Martial cannot repeat his name often enough.

✢ ✢ ✢

Hermes, favourite fighter of the day…Hermes, skilled with every weapon, Hermes, both gladiator and doctor, Hermes the Hurricane, terror of his ludus, Hermes, who frightens Helius (and is the only man who can), Hermes, who knocks down Advolans (and is the only man who can)…Hermes, the ticket scalper's gold-mine, Hermes, the darling and heart-breaker of his female groupies, Hermes, proud with martial spear, Hermes, threatening with the trident, Hermes, fearsome with trailing helmet, Hermes, the glory of all kinds of war, Hermes, everything in himself, and three times unique.

MARTIAL *EPIGRAMS* 5.24

✢ ✢ ✢

Other suggestions include:

Felix 'Happy' or 'fortunate'
Hilarus 'The cheerful'
Narcissus Another mythological character
Nikephorus 'Bearer of victory' (Greek)
Victor For straightforward Latin types
Maximus 'The greatest' – for those who feel Victor is too subtle

Asiaticus For someone from Asia Minor
Sabinus From the Sabine country of Italy
Flamma 'The flame'
Cygnus 'The swan'
Mansuetus 'The polite', for those with a sense of irony
Florus 'Blossom' (ditto)

Those really keen on anonymity choose generic, everyday names, so common that they are highly forgettable, such as:

Valerius
Sergius
Valens
Servius
Servilius

Those bearing a single name are often slaves, so some *auctorati*, even if they forswear their real names, might still use a two-part name such as Lucius Pompeius or Marcus Rutilius. Some even advertise that they are Roman citizens, as did Marcus Quintus Ducenius, who proudly uses his distinctive three-part Roman name, the *tria nomina*, on the same tombstone that boasts of his arena victories.

Those with but a single name will find the lack compensated for by the use of their chosen speciality, with the name of the *familia gladiatoria* completing the identification. So a graffito praising *Hilarus Ner. XI v) XIII* clearly identifies Hilarus of the Neronian family, who has won nine times in the thirteen combats he has survived.

M. Attilius the beginner takes on the experienced Hilarus. Probably to his own surprise, Attilius emerges as the victor. (This is shown by the 'V' which finishes the line.)

Choosing a speciality

Some gladiator types, such as the Gaul or Samnite, are now out of fashion, but plenty of choices remain. As well as choosing the name, the *magister* and *lanista* must decide on the role for which their tiro is best suited. They may even consult the individual whose future depends on their choice, but don't bet on it.

Statuettes of provocator-style gladiators. With everything aligned for combat, helmet, shield and greaves present a solidly armoured front to an opponent.

- - - - - - - - - - -

Heavies

A physically powerful type with (relatively) limited agility will probably end up in the heavy squad. This is a generic name for several types of gladiator, properly called the *scutarii*, or 'shield carriers'). These are gladiators who fight with a sword, large shield and a considerable amount of armour, including that anonymizing helmet. Soldiers and ex-soldiers take a particular interest in these types, as their kit is the closest to actual legionary equipment. Since legionaries are encouraged to watch gladiator fights to get them used to bloodletting, soldiers will be a discerning part of a heavy's audience, especially in provincial amphitheatres. Types of 'heavy' include:

Provocator 'The challenger'

Weapon – a short sword (sometimes a short, short sword).
Shield – large, rectangular. A superior version of legionary issue.
Helmet – all-encompassing, with grille-covered eyeholes for visibility.
Armour – *manica* (protective sleeve), greave (protecting the forward leg) and *cardiophylax* (chest protector).
Usual opponent – another *provocator*.

Anyone who uses a shield purely for defence is missing half the weapon's potential. In this mosaic from Germania, a gladiator demonstrates this powerfully.

Murmillo 'The fish man'

Weapon – short sword.

Shield – large, wooden, partly oval or rectangular.

Helmet – full face, with the distinctive crest that might look like a 'fish-fin' from some angles.

Armour – padded or armoured guard on the sword arm, protective greave.

Usual opponent – Thracian, though smaller arenas might also match a *murmillo* with a *provocator* or *retiarius* (though the *murmillo*'s helmet is so vulnerable to a good net cast that the latter is not really a fair fight).

Secutor 'The chaser'

Weapon – short sword and a dagger as back-up.

Shield – large, wooden, rectangular.

Helmet – full face, smooth and egg-shaped, with few projections a net can catch on.

Armour – padded or armoured guard on the sword arm, protective greave.

Usual opponent – *retiarius*. In fact, chasing the nimble *retiarius* gives the *secutor* his name.

Small-shield fighters (parmularii)

Sometimes it pays to be agile. A lightly armoured fighter can skip around his more cumbersome opponent looking for an opening. Also, while the heavies are limited to a sword, and sometimes a rather limited sword at that, the lighter fighters are equipped with a variety of items to ruin an opponent's day. Types of *parmularii* include:

FROM TOP TO BOTTOM *A* murmillo *takes a bow after his combat; a* secutor *prepares to finish off a* retiarius; *and two* parmularii *adopt fighting poses as they measure up the opposition.*

Hoplomachus 'The hoplite fighter'
Weapon – thrusting spear, short sword
and dagger.
Shield – round, small, curved. Generally
made of metal, such as bronze.
Helmet – Grecian style, as a nod to the
original hoplite opponents of Rome.
Armour – padded or armoured
guard on the sword arm and thigh,
protective greave.
Usual opponent – *murmillo* or
Thracian.

Thracian
Weapon – curved Thracian dagger, about a foot long.
Shield – small, curved and rectangular.
Helmet – distinctive, wide-brimmed, often with a griffin. (Griffins
were the companions of Nemesis, goddess of impending doom.)
Armour – padded arm and thigh guards and greave.
Usual opponent – *murmillo* or *hoplomachus*.

Retiarius 'The net-man'
Weapon – a trident and a net, dagger as back-up.
Shield – the *galerus*, armour fitted to the shoul-
der as part of the arm-guard. One part flares
up and protects the neck on that side.
Helmet – none.
Armour – padded arm-guard on the
non-trident-carrying arm.
Usual opponent – *secutor*.

- -

TOP *The metal shield of a* hoplomachus *deflects an opposing Samnite's thrust
over his shoulder, and he prepares a counter-strike.*

ABOVE *During a break from the action, a* retiarius *holds what appears
to be a rolled-up net in his hands.*

Eques 'The horseman'
Weapon – lance and short sword.
Shield – *parma equestris,* the small
cavalry shield.
Helmet – old-style brimmed
cavalry type.
Armour – padding on right arm.
Usual opponent – because they start
the combat on horseback, *equites*
only fight their own kind. However,
after the initial horsing around,
the *equites* generally dismount and
finish their business on foot.

After sparring on horseback, two equites
dismount and finish the combat on foot.

Speciality fighters

The *editores* who present the games are always on the lookout for novelty. There are also advantages in being an unusual class of fighter, because while such gladiators are experienced in facing the regular arena types, the regulars don't know what they are up against. Some of the most common uncommon types are:

Andabata The *andabatae* have helmets without eyeholes, so that they fight without being able to see their opponent. For obvious reasons they only fight other *andabatae*. Hilariously lethal, if that's your idea of fun.

Dimachaerus A fighter with two swords and no shield. For those who believe that attack is the best form of defence.

Essedarius A chariot fighter in the old Celtic tradition. Popular a hundred years ago, but now rare.

Laquearius Basically a *retiarius* with a lasso. The type is very rare and will probably never really catch on.

Helmet of a Thracian gladiator. These helmets are often topped with an ornamental griffin crest, for griffins draw the chariot of Nemesis. In practical terms, the griffin means that a Thracian must duck further and faster to completely avoid a blow.

'Parade armour'. These showy greaves (leg-warmers for gladiators) depict a gladiatorial dilemma – should one go with sensible armour that allows one to fight better, or slightly impractical kit that will impress the audience?

In this mosaic from the province of Africa, five venatores (beast-fighters) carouse at an arena-shaped table with their future victims before them. Each venator carries the symbol of his particular guild. A worried slave rushes over with finger to his lips saying, 'Quiet – let the bulls sleep!'

The importance of shields as advertising is shown in this mosaic of equites.
Regrettably, Maternus has no further use for his. The theta symbol by his name shows
that his wound is fatal.

The mosaic shows the inscriptions: ASTANAX VICIT, KALENDIO Ø (upper panel) and ASTANAX, KALENDIO Ø (lower panel).

ABOVE *Astanax the* secutor *v. Kalendio the* retiarius. *This mosaic shows that Kalendio successfully cast his net over the* secutor, *but even so he could not stop Astanax from making his kill.*

OPPOSITE *Death in the arena. This 1st-century BC bas-relief shows a gladiator being finished off by his opponent. Since then, gladiator equipment has become more elaborate, and the fighters are now armoured against minor wounds.*

Bruised and bleeding, a gladiator slumps to the sand during a training bout. His opponent, a Nubian retiarius, lies prone, his trident cast aside. This mosaic, from the Villa Wadi Lebda, near Leptis Magna, Tunisia, dating to 2nd century AD, has carefully depicted the different muscle formations in the gladiator's sword and shield arms.

Riot in Pompeii (see page 161). The pitched battle between Pompeians and Nucerians in AD 59 represents one of the few times when it was safer to be in the arena than in the spectators' seats. The Pompeians won, but were harshly punished afterwards.

Practical anatomy

The physician Galen remarked that the best school for a surgeon is the battlefield, though a gladiatorial school comes a close second. Only in these places do doctors get a close look at the workings of the human anatomy while they are still working, at least temporarily. It behooves a gladiator who wants to walk out of the arena likewise to acquaint himself with the human body. A few fingers' breadth can make the difference between an opponent infuriated by his wound and one dead from it. A strictly non-medicinal anatomy course will consider the following aspects.

Major organs

The thoughtful gladiator will carefully note the length of his sword, and the fact that there are very few vital organs of the body that a correctly inserted blade of more than four inches cannot penetrate – and even the short sword of a *provocator* is at least twice this length. However, 'vital' is a relative term when referring to organs. The only immediate kills come from injuries to the heart and brain.

Nature has made the same observation, and armoured the brain with the bony helmet of the skull and located the heart under the solid sternum, providing that organ with the protection that gladiator equipment has carefully neglected to provide. (Gladiators are well protected from minor wounds, but are deliberately exposed to killing blows.) If stabbing for the heart through the ribcage, remember to turn the blade sideways, since otherwise only the tip goes in and the blade jams between the ribs. However, at the point of the arch of the ribs an upward stab can reach the heart very handily. Also note that a somewhat straighter and deeper stab to the same point has a good chance of severing the aorta or the vena cava, which run against the spine.

Likewise, though both nature and helmet have armoured the gladiator's head, a solid upward stab through the soft tissue under the chin will probably make it to the brain stem. Just take care to avoid the helmet chinstrap.

Arteries and veins

Again, nature has carefully tucked these vulnerable points deep within the protection of the body, but the design of human anatomy means that major blood vessels are occasionally exposed. The subclavian artery is too well protected to interest a gladiator, and most helmets are careful to shield the jugular and carotid. However, the junction of the jugular and innominate veins just below where the throat meets the ribcage is accessible to a quick probing downward stab. And even more attractive are the brachial and axillary vessels, through which you can feel the blood pumping if you tuck your fingers into your armpit – and how do you armour an armpit?

Also, do not forget the femoral artery, armoured on the outside by the basin of the hip-bone but vulnerable to an inward stab above the groin, where even if you miss there's a chance of slicing the great saphenous vein. Note that even if an opponent protects his major vulnerabilities, a series of minor wounds will eventually cause debilitation from blood loss, so cut and nick whenever possible.

Connective tissue

Muscle has been designed by nature to take a lot of punishment, and sticking a weapon into it is generally not worth the effort, since every strike makes the attacker vulnerable to a better-aimed counter-strike. However, there are several exceptions, provided one remembers the rule that one stabs for vital organs and slashes at connective tissue. For example, the stomach muscles are not themselves essential organs, but they hold the intestines in place (until slashed open). Gladiators like the very wide metal belt (*balteus*) which guards against this eventuality. This belt also means that anyone with a heavy enough sword must aim for the small space between belt and ribs if aiming to cut the spine.

Leg guards give some protection, but an opponent can still be slowed down if his hamstrings are cut by a slash across the back of the knee. A blow that crushes the larynx or the accompanying cartilage causes the injured organ to swell up and block the trachea, causing a quick death by suffocation.

Overall, a trained gladiator tends to see the human body as irrelevant flesh surrounding a number of crucial vulnerabilities. For non-gladiators this can actually be rather good news. Rome is a rough place. Many who meet a gladiator in the course of business outside the arena are being persuaded of the need to repay their debts at any cost, or are otherwise discovering that the hirer of the gladiators is extremely displeased with them. Those being beaten to within an inch of their lives can find a certain reassurance in knowing the job is being done by professionals who know where and precisely how hard to hit – and when to stop hitting. If they do beat someone to death, at least it won't be accidental.

Case study I: The making of a *provocator*

A *provocator* fights carrying about 30 pounds of equipment in all. For a large, fit fighter, the weight is less of a problem than the fact that the helmet, body protection and shield significantly restrict both mobility and visibility. Above all, a *provocator* rapidly develops a love-hate relationship with his helmet.

A distinctive signature piece, protector of anonymity, and defender of the cranium, the helmet is also hot, suffocating and neck-wrenchingly heavy. For all the advantages helmets give the wearer, few gladiators love their headgear.

The helmet
This provides excellent protection, making the head virtually invulnerable to most attacks. Since people locate their conscious selves at a point about four inches back from the eyes, a protected head is a great confidence booster. But it comes at a price.

It's dehumanizing A gladiator in a helmet is deliberately made a faceless killing machine. This can help to intimidate an opponent, but it also makes it easier for someone (perhaps even someone you shared a drink with a few hours ago) to see you as un-human and easier to kill without qualms.

It's confining Any *provocator* knows that it's usually five seconds after the helmet is fitted that an unscratchable itch develops on the edge of his nose. But an itch goes away when more pressing concerns arise. Sweat trickling into your eyes is much more serious when you can't just brush it away, so ensure the helmet's padding can absorb lots of moisture.

It makes breathing difficult Even a trained gladiator gets out of breath in a *provocator* helmet. In fact, a trained gladiator gets out of breath faster, because his body sucks in a larger amount of oxygen. More, in fact, than the airholes can provide.

It dangerously restricts visibility In smaller arenas a *provocator* may sometimes fight other gladiator types. Here, a favourite trick of the *retiarius* is to trail his net on the ground, knowing that the *provocator's* helmet does not allow the fighter to look down to see where he is treading. In a large arena, the well-prepared *provocator* will carefully locate all trapdoors on the fighting surface. They never manage to get the blasted things exactly flush with the ground, and sometimes stumbling over a trapdoor edge can really ruin your day.

Because visibility is so limited, the *provocator* is trained not to take his eyes off his opponent no matter what. Many a gladiator who failed to do this has died literally never knowing what hit him. Watch your opponent, and let your other senses take care of the rest.

As a result of all these factors, unless anonymity is absolutely essential, his helmet is the last thing a *provocator* puts on before going into action, and the first thing he takes off.

Feet

Though relatively well-armoured for a gladiator, the *provocator*, like other gladiators, fights barefoot. Anyone who has ever walked along a beach wearing sandals will quickly work out why. Sand behind the heel and between the toes rapidly becomes a crippling distraction.

A *provocator* has an additional reason for fighting barefoot. That's because his toes tell him about the surface underfoot which his helmet won't let him see. The *provocator* is trained to approach an opponent by sliding each foot forward along the ground. This helps to maintain stance and balance, but also gives warning of nasty surprises (such as nets) lurking unseen underfoot.

The shield

For the *provocator* in his faceless helmet, a shield is more than body protection; it's even more than an auxiliary offensive weapon (though it performs both these tasks excellently). A shield is advertising space. It's somewhere to show a distinctive personality, something that allows a particular fighter to be immediately recognized by the crowd. Features such as triple-ply oiled oak construction with iron rims top and bottom come as standard in any good *ludus*. What the *provocator* agonizes over is the motif and colour scheme on the front. Ideally this should both impress the crowd and terrify an opponent (or, since a gladiator doesn't terrify easily, at least remind him of his mortality with an image of Nemesis, or Cerberus, the hell-hound he might soon be meeting).

The best defence is attack Shields are not just for hiding behind. Generally, the grip is right in the middle. It lies sideways so that one holds the shield 'suitcase-style', as though the handle is a knuckleduster clenched in a closed fist. Indeed, a well-trained gladiator can punch startlingly hard and fast with a shield. Another form of 'shield-bash' is when the gladiator makes a sudden rush to hit an off-balance opponent with his full body weight behind the shield.

Getting edgy Generally, one does not want the shield too far from one's body, which is why an opponent constantly tries to 'open' the shield by pulling it away from the *provocator* at an angle (a *retiarius*'s trident is good at this). However, occasionally in mid-melee it helps to give someone a good whack somewhere vulnerable with a shield edge (or better, a shield corner). And then there's the 'shield drop'. This is when, going toe-to-toe with an opponent, you drop your whole body into a crouch and slam your metal shield edge down hard on his vulnerable bare tootsies.

Swords take second place to shields as offensive weapons here. The middle gladiator steps under a shield slamming at his face, and bangs his own shield down hard on his opponent's toes.

Taking the weight off A shield is heavy, and after a few minutes the way it is carried makes it a weight even for over-developed gladiatorial biceps. So except in a crisis, it's a good idea to rest the bottom edge of the shield against the protective greave of the left leg. One can even advance in that position, with the left leg kept forward and shuffled along the ground, so that an opponent sees mostly the shield advancing inexorably, with only small bits of gladiator showing behind.

Graffiti of gladiators in action at Nola in Italy. As togaed spectators look on, musicians (far right) play rousing music.

- -

The sword

If you're lucky, you'll get about a foot and a half of blade. Training with the sword is constant, and a gladiator is trained to know exactly where the sword tip is at any given moment. Fighting with a short sword is utterly unlike fencing with a long one. Sword-to-sword is rare.

One stab is better than three slashes Eighteen inches might not sound a lot, but you only need to insert a quarter of that into an opponent if you pick your target. If you have a well-sharpened weapon – and many gladiators prefer to sharpen their own – it takes a surprisingly gentle push to get a blade into most parts of the body. (You don't want to do a really hard stab, because blades embedded in bone are hard to pull out.) Therefore a quick attack (which is more a coordinated series of moves than a single stab) is the order of the day, and if it fails, go back to the guard position and await another chance.

Now you see it… The shorter blade has one advantage. It's easy to keep it behind the shield with just the tip showing, or even hidden completely, so that an opponent is unsure of the angle of attack. Then a lightning attack, followed by a quick revert to the initial position, and it's easy to get an opponent off-guard and uncertain.

Case study II: The making of a *retiarius*

The position of the net-man is an ambiguous anomaly in the otherwise rigid hierarchy of the *ludus*. For some, the *retiarius* is the lowest of the lot, since he fights without a helmet, with his face and his shame clear for all to see. For others the *retiarius* is actually more prestigious, as of all arena fighters, he relies most on his skill and courage for victory. There is a theory that while an average *secutor* will beat an average *retiarius* eight times out of ten, a really good *retiarius* will beat a skilled *secutor* by the same margin. (Though you won't get many *secutores* agreeing with this proposition.)

This drawing from a Spanish mosaic shows a secutor *struggling to free himself from a successful net cast in the few moments remaining before the* retiarius *brings his trident into play.*

- - - - - - - - - - -

The role of *retiarius* is also favoured by some who like to fight in the arena as non-professionals, just to show off their skill at arms. The lack of a helmet makes it clear exactly who is doing the fighting. On the other hand, since a *retiarius*'s equipment is so different from standard military gear, even ex-soldiers must learn how to use it from scratch.

The net

The problem with a net is that it is generally a one-shot weapon. Once it is cast, half the *retiarius*'s offensive capability has gone with the throw. A miss, and you have a half-naked man with a trident against an armoured opponent whose morale has just improved. On the other hand, a really good throw so incapacitates an opponent that it is game over, with victory to the *retiarius*. So a *retiarius* in training spends an awful amount of time learning how and when to make that all-important throw. It's no use just draping the net over an opponent, for example, if you don't tangle him up thoroughly while you are at it.

Dangerous by design Though his kit comes from that of a fisherman, neither a gladiator's trident nor his net would be much good for catching fish. (Fish-men, such as the *murmillo* fighter, are another matter.) Years of experience have taught the *ludus* net-makers the optimal weave that will allow weapons, swords or helmets to get well entangled. Large holes are better in the centre of the net, with a finer mesh at the edges. Larger holes are better for tangling, and a finer mesh at the edges makes the net heavier there. Because it is heavier at the rim, the net does not need weights to open properly when cast.

It's all in the wrist A proper cast needs a nifty arm and wrist action, a sort of circular movement which sends the net spinning slowly as it flies towards its target. The spin transfers centrifugal force to the edges, thus fully opening the net. Because different parts of the net stop spinning at different times when it has landed on something, this helps to tangle everything up nicely. A veteran gladiator can drop his net over a target 30 feet away. This is not a good idea, however, since a net in flight takes easily four seconds to cover this distance – and an able *secutor* can catch a quick nap or exchange a few words of gossip with a friend and still leave himself time to step aside.

Get it right first time The ideal throwing distance varies from *retiarius* to *retiarius*, which is one reason why a heavy paired against a net-man will be well advised to take any chance to study his opponent in action before they meet in combat. Most net-men prefer to throw the net just two or three yards, and some do their cast at very close range with one hand wrapped in the folds of the net so they don't lose it even if a throw goes wrong.

Staying with the net There is also the possibility of having the net on a tether so it can be pulled back if a throw misses. This is not a good idea, however, because the tether interferes with the rotatory action of a smooth deployment. Also, if throwing any distance (rather than draping the net over an opponent when up close), a net is a fire-and-forget weapon. Most *secutores* will attack immediately after a throw, and a *retiarius* pre-occupied with getting his net back is a *retiarius* unable to deal with more pressing concerns.

Happy endings An empty net thumping on to the sand represents a fail for the *retiarius*. Snagging any part of an opponent will discombobulate him at least temporarily, and an able net-man will immediately exploit the options for attack that the net has opened up. A cast in which the net completely envelops the body and sword of an opponent is ideal. A *retiarius* smiling in his sleep at night is probably dreaming of that perfect cast in which head and sword are inextricably tangled with each other, and the *secutor* has no choice but to struggle to free one finger long enough to plead with the crowd for mercy.

The trident

This is the *retiarius*'s main offensive weapon. Its three teeth (which is what 'tri-dent' means) are very different from those used by a fisherman. First, the prongs are shorter (remember, more than 4 inches is unnecessary), though some *retiarii* favour a trident with a middle prong almost half as long again as the others. Secondly, the prongs are not barbed. A fisherman does not want his fish to slip off the end of his barbed trident, but the last thing a net-man wants is to have his principal striking weapon irretrievably stuck in the thigh of an opponent. It is also harder than it appears to keep the prongs of the trident from getting tangled in the net, and barbed prongs would make untangling impossible.

Mix it up Variety is the spice of the *retiarius*'s bag of tricks. Sometimes he will stab overhand, using the superior reach of the trident to hit the helmet and shoulder of an opponent. Catching the top of the shield might allow the *retiarius* his prime ambition – to 'open' his opponent by peeling his shield away from his body. Underhand stabs aim at the sword hand, the torso and the top of the thigh. A well-trained net-man might even use his trident as a quarter-staff, swinging the butt-end to good effect. (However, unlike a staff, the trident is not balanced, and its solidity makes it heavy and hard to swing fast.) Ideally, a *secutor* should have no idea of what the *retiarius*'s next attack will be or what angle it will come from.

Trip him up There are two techniques for this. If a *secutor* makes a rush, sometimes all it takes is the trident poked in front of his back foot, and down he goes.

The second method is more complicated and requires a lot of practice. There's also the risk of losing the trident. Make several fast thrusts at the helmet of the *secutor*, forcing him to raise his guard. Then move the trident swiftly down and hack behind the ankle of his front foot and pull. Your opponent will momentarily be off-balance. While he is teetering on one leg, you have less than a second to hit his helmet again – this time very hard – and so bring him down. Alternatively, you can try a body charge. If you succeed the *secutor* will go down, and a well-trained *retiarius* will make sure he never gets up.

Break it up A *secutor* standing on balance with all his kit aligned is almost impossible to defeat. So the job of the *retiarius* is to get his opponent off-balance, with his body unshielded, and his sword wrongly deployed. He does this by breaking down his opponent's composure with quick stabs and feints, constantly changing the angle of attack and relying on the fact that eventually his opponent's relatively limited mobility and vision will lead him to make a mistake. Just don't count on getting a second chance.

Flexibility and mobility

The *galerus* (arm and shoulder guard) is not the main protection of the *retiarius*. Mobility is. Fighting toe-to-toe with the well-armoured and well-equipped *secutor* is suicide, so a net-man has to rely on his mobility and his wits. At the beginning the *secutor* will aim to finish the fight with a single well-aimed thrust of his sword. The job of the *retiarius* is not to be there when that stab happens. More than most gladiators, he is grateful for the shape of the arena. You can't get cornered in a place that doesn't have corners, and the longer the fight goes on, the more the *secutor* will tire. Being aware that his advantage is slipping away, he is more likely to make mistakes.

Note: The writer particularly thanks Cerberus (*retiarius*) and Medusa (*provocatorix*) (a.k.a. Alexander and Svenja) of the Ludus Nemesis for sharing their hands-on experience.

Codex Gladiorum

There was a Pompeian gladiator called Jesus, presumably a man of Jewish origin.

✠

Left-handed legionaries are strongly discouraged. But a left-handed gladiator has the edge on someone accustomed to fighting fellow righties.

✠

While other gladiators fight bare-chested, *equites* traditionally have sleeveless tunics.

✠

If a trident does get entangled in a net, the *retiarius* might decide to throw the lot over an opponent, and leave him with the task of disentangling the trident. This is especially effective if the *retiarius* is allowed a smaller secondary weapon such as a dagger.

✠

A *retiarius* might also 'open' his opponent's guard by kicking the bottom of his shield hard, and then, as the top tips forward, wrenching it away with the trident.

✠

A gladiator helmet is about twice the weight of an infantry helmet. The *secutor*'s helmet must resist the thrusts of a trident and, therefore, is even thicker and heavier.

✠

A later historian (Ammianus) refers to Sassanian Persian infantry as 'sheltering behind their shields as *murmillos* do' – a reference to the murmillian belief that defence is the best form of attack.

✠

A murmillo *helmet, with its traditional 'fish-fin' crest.*

- - - - - - - - - - - - - - - - - -

✦ VI ✦
Gladiators Outside the Arena

A free man wants nothing others can give, for otherwise he is their slave.

HANDBOOK OF EPICTETUS THE STOIC 14

✦ ✦ ✦

While gladiators have their major effect on Roman life through their performances in shows and spectacles, these spectacles are relatively infrequent events. There are many – including bored and wealthy women – who in various ways find useful employment for these fine bodies of men when they are not fighting or training.

Gladiators as soldiers

There is a close connection between soldiers and gladiators. After all, both are essentially trained killers, and military spectators are keenly appreciative of the subtleties of gladiatorial combat. Occasionally – and usually in times of crisis – the boot is on the other foot, and gladiators get to have a go at being soldiers.

At first glance, this would seem a reasonable idea, since a commander looking for skilled fighters would be seriously remiss if he did not consider enrolling a corps of men who are in top physical condition and have spent years honing their skills at hand-to-hand combat. Furthermore, the Romans have rueful memories of the late 70s BC, when the renegade gladiator Spartacus and his men spent several years beating up whatever regular troops the Romans sent against them.

Yet the legions got Spartacus in the end, and there is a negative side to enlisting gladiators, for there is more to being a soldier than fighting. For example, gladiators are used to being waited upon by the support staff at their *ludus*. Foraging for food and cooking what one finds is a black art to the gladiator, who expects his food pre-cooked (in large portions) and delivered to his plate at regular intervals. Individualists to a man, gladiators have neither the training nor inclination for group manoeuvres and are better at fighting each other than fighting as a unit. In fact, gladiators are pretty poor soldiers except in a disorganized melee, where they are truly formidable.

Soldiers on parade. Behind the pomp and splendour, it's not unknown for a general to have a personal bodyguard of gladiators to help keep order in the ranks.

During the civil wars that followed the death of Nero in AD 68, the biographer Plutarch tells us that gladiators were used to garrison the town of Tarracina (about 50 miles southeast of Rome). Their experience was fairly typical of what could be expected of gladiators at war. Military matters such as patrols and sentry duty were passed over in favour of partying and debauchery, but when the inevitable happened and regular troops stormed the city, gladiators were among the few who stood their ground, and 'sold their lives dearly'.

There is also the fact that, as Tacitus remarks, gladiators are 'shameful assistants' in a campaign. Recruiting slaves or gladiators (and many gladiators were slaves anyway) is generally seen as a sign of desperation, and suggests that a commander cannot get enough decent Roman citizens behind his cause. Therefore, gladiators are usually recruited during civil wars, when any kind of fighting skill is urgently required. Some of the best-known examples include:

Decimus Brutus who had a substantial corps of gladiators with him when he successfully defended Mutina (later Modena) from Mark Antony in 44 BC after the assassination of Julius Caesar. This same Decimus Brutus had provided the gladiators who gave armed support to the assassins immediately after they had stabbed Caesar, and the defenders of Mutina may have included many of the same men.

When **Octavian and Lepidus** joined with Mark Antony to form the Triumvirate (three men who tried to rule the Roman empire as colleagues), gladiators were among a commando force of legionaries and light-armed troops that resisted their rule and attacked the south Italian port of Brundisium.

Mark Antony and his brother Lucius were often called 'gladiators' by their enemy Cicero. 'I call Antony a gladiator as a term of abuse,' the orator explained, 'but for his brother I'm simply using plain Latin'. (This is because Lucius allegedly performed as a gladiator in a show in Asia Minor.) Both Antonys used gladiators in their struggle with Octavian as the triumvirate fell apart.

Lucius used gladiators in his unsuccessful attempt to unseat Octavian from power in Italy. When he was driven from Rome, his gladiators were instrumental in seizing the city of Perusia, further up the river Tiber. When Octavian came to besiege the city, the historian Appian tells us 'he had the better missile troops, but Lucius's gladiators were much better at hand-to-hand fighting and caused many casualties'. It was at this siege that gladiators nearly changed history. Octavian ventured too near the walls for comfort, and an unexpected sally by the gladiators came close to depriving the Roman empire of its future Augustus.

Antony began collecting gladiators in the city of Cyzicus while he was still at war with Octavian. In a rare moment of forethought (and a typical moment of hubris) he considered that he needed a decent spectacle prepared beforehand to celebrate his eventual triumph over his rival. Instead Antony was soundly defeated at Actium in 31 BC. He fled to Egypt, and the band of gladiators he had assembled decided to fight their way south to join him. King Herod of Judaea sent troops to prevent this (though he is better known for sending troops to slay his considerably less formidable infant 'enemies' in Bethlehem). Eventually the gladiators surrendered on the promise of being enrolled in the legions, but instead the hopeful recruits were split into small groups and then executed.

The reign of the emperor **Claudius** saw an example of gladiators and soldiers working together, but in this case the enemy was not hostile troops, but a large fire which threatened to engulf the Roman forum.

Under the short-lived emperor **Otho** gladiators made a spectacular return to the battlefield in the civil wars that followed the death of Nero. Otho recruited the contents of the imperial *ludi* in Rome, and took 2,000 gladiators north to fight a rival near Cremona in AD 69. At first the gladiators were successful, chopping an opposing unit of auxiliary soldiers into dogmeat. Later, an enemy unit of water-wise Batavian auxiliary soldiers caught the gladiators making a river crossing. They briskly destroyed both transports and gladiators before they reached the opposite bank.

Once the solid and pragmatic **Vespasian** had taken the imperial purple, peace returned. Gladiators were again relegated to fighting in the arena, and there they have stayed, thanks to the peace that has blessed the civic life of the empire throughout the following century.

The emperor Vespasian, restorer of peace in AD 70, founder of the Flavian dynasty. Known to gladiators mainly as the builder of the Flavian Amphitheatre, the world's all-time premier fighting venue, where thousands of men and tens of thousands of animals have since perished.

Gladiators in the house

✛ ✛ ✛

*He lived with a household of actors and gladiators, the former to abet
his lusts, the latter to abet his crimes.*

CICERO *ON STANDING FOR CONSUL* 3
(WRITING TO HIS BROTHER QUINTUS ABOUT A POLITICAL RIVAL)

✛ ✛ ✛

Gladiators might train in the *ludus*, but they do not always live there.
Blaesus, proconsul of Pannonia in AD 14, had slave gladiators in his retinue
while he was commander of the army, and used these men to discipline
recalcitrant soldiers. Even when in Rome many wealthy senators and equestrians have found it useful to have a gladiator or two on the premises. This
is not simply so that unwelcome petitioners can be ejected with extreme
force, but also because gladiators act as personal trainers for a senate whose
members still take skill at arms very seriously. Julius Caesar used to do this
the other way around, billeting his younger gladiators at the homes of experienced military men and urging them to practise duelling against each
other and so mutually improve their skills. When the head of the household
goes out into the forum, his gladiators accompany him as bodyguards for
his esteemed person and as visible proof that he is rich enough to afford
such trappings of power.

In these peaceful days a gladiator on bodyguard duty will probably
appear simply as an over-muscled Roman, with – at most – a vest of chain
mail jingling gently under his tunic. Two centuries ago, in the disturbed
days at the end of the Republic, gladiator bodyguards were a lot more
blatant about it.

The tribune **Caius Cato** (a distant relative of Cato the Younger) acquired a
number of gladiators and Cicero remarked to his brother that 'he never
appeared in public without them in their complete panoply of armour.
However, he could not afford to maintain them, and had trouble keeping
the troupe together'. Eventually, to Cato's chagrin, the gladiators were
purchased by a rival.

Clodius, a bitter rival of Cicero, used gladiators to protect not just his person but also his political ambitions. When he successfully had Cicero exiled, Clodius borrowed gladiators from his brother Appius Claudius and used them to disrupt the people's assemblies that gathered to vote for the orator's recall. We have already seen how Clodius's gladiators were outmatched by those of his rival Milo, who killed the turbulent politician on the Appian Way outside Rome (p. 35).

Decimus Brutus, as we have seen above, provided gladiators to his relative Marcus Brutus to beef up the efforts of Caesar's assassins. These gladiators were stationed under arms near the assassination site on the pretext that they were practising for a show, and after the killing they withdrew with the 'liberators' to guard their refuge on the Capitoline Hill.

Emperors continued the tradition of gladiators frequenting the houses of the wealthy.

Nero had as his favourite the gladiator Spiculus, who picked up some of the spoils when Nero executed his senatorial enemies (real or imagined). When Rome tired of the tyrant emperor, Nero turned to Spiculus to end his life. But Spiculus had already fled the imperial household, though it did him little good. He was caught by the mob, who, with a fine Roman sense of irony, crushed him under a statue of Nero as they pulled it down.

Caligula practised hand-to-hand combat with a gladiator trainer, and when beating one in a duel allegedly went on to kill his man. This did not apparently disturb those gladiators whom Caligula made officers of his German bodyguard – a bodyguard that remained loyal even when the praetorians turned against the emperor and abetted his assassination.

The tyrant Nero made members of senatorial families fight in the arena to shame them, and perhaps to make his own appearances on stage respectable by comparison.

Domitian's gladiators were also loyal, but to his chamberlain Parthenius, who (by some accounts) ordered in half a dozen of them to finish off his imperial master when Domitian appeared to be getting the better of the assassin sent against him.

Roman dinner party. Once the tables were cleared, postprandial entertainment might be anything from poetry readings to lewd displays by dancing girls or a demonstration gladiator bout.

Gladiators might make an appearance towards the end of an upper-class dinner party and change the cut-and-thrust of postprandial discussion to some cutting and thrusting of a more literal variety. Generally these fights are exhibition matches, in which either wooden swords or blunted weapons are used. Anyone taking part in such an event is expected to give value for money (and the money is often very good), so at best participants expect to get off with some livid bruises. On the other hand, this is nothing worse than one might get from some exceptionally hard sparring in the *ludus*, and if there are lots of leftovers from the dinner party, there's a chance of getting a really good meal out of it as well.

One of the advantages of being very wealthy is that one seldom gets one's own hands dirty. So rich people without gladiators in their household can still use them as enforcers – but in a strictly non-attributable manner. If multi-millionaire Sextus Nefarius wants to buy out a family farmstead right in the middle of his planned new country estate, he certainly won't hand over a few purses of gold to the local gladiator school. He knows that almost everything that happens is witnessed by some household servant, and such servants can be questioned by an over-zealous magistrate.

No, instead Sextus gives the purses to the major-domo of his household, and explains that he has a problem with the farmstead. The major-domo goes to someone who regularly hires the gladiators for the games, and explains the nature of the problem. Later, when Sextus is taken to task because the head of the farming household has been beaten to a pulp by a gang of burly gladiators, he can profess his horror at this unfortunate mis-understanding, and offer to buy the farmstead at a very generous price, since the farmsteader is no longer capable of working it.

The triumvir Crassus was a Roman of the old school who knew how to make a subtle threat. One complicated squabble was resolved when, as Cicero explained in a letter to his friend Atticus, 'Old Baldy [Crassus] settled the whole business with just one slave acting for him – a clerk from a gladia-tor school'. If Crassus could send a clerk from a gladiator school, he could send other, even more persuasive individuals from that school, an inference that evidently did not escape the other parties to the discussion.

Gladiators in the boudoir

✛ ✛ ✛

It was believed that Nymphidius [an imperial pretender] was
a son of Martianus the gladiator with whom his mother fell in love
because of his fame.

PLUTARCH *LIFE OF GALBA* 9

✛ ✛ ✛

When Eppia, the senator's wife, ran off with a gladiator
To Pharos and the Nile and the ill-famed city of Lagus,
Canopus itself cried shame upon the monstrous morals of our town.
Forgetful of home, of husband and of sister, without thought
of her motherland,
She shamelessly abandoned her weeping children,
And more amazing yet, she abandoned the [gladiatorial] games.

And what were the youthful charms which captivated Eppia?
What did she see in him to allow herself to be called a gladiator-groupie?
Her dear Sergius had…a wounded arm promising to discharge pus,

His face had various deformities, from a scar caused by the helmet,
To a huge cyst upon his nose, a nasty fluid always trickling from his eye.
But hey, he was a gladiator!

It is this that transforms these fellows into [the beautiful youth of myth] Hyacinth.
This is what she prefers to children and to country, to sister and to husband.
What such women love is his impaling instrument *
But had this Sergius been discharged from the arena,
He would have been no better to her than [her husband] Veiento.

JUVENAL *SATIRES* 6

✛ ✛ ✛

For better or worse, gladiators are sexy, though it deeply pains writers like Juvenal that many women favour the sweaty musculature of an arena fighter over the highly evolved sensitivity of a poet. Gladiators and their *lanistae* are well aware of this fact. Many a wealthy lady who hires gladiator bodyguards for a night does so in the expectation of her body being guarded very closely indeed. The slave girl Chrysis in the *Satyricon* of Petronius remarks sourly of her 'betters' that 'there are those who can only get on heat with the absolute dregs…the arena certainly does it for some'.

The lady and the gladiator. For legal reasons we cannot confirm or deny any relationship between this wealthy matron from Egypt and the over-muscled gladiator with the low forehead on her left.

* *Gladius* had a double meaning for Romans.

Messalina, the wife of the emperor Claudius, was certainly among the ladies referred to, but if popular reports about the nymphomaniac empress are to be believed, being a gladiator was not absolutely necessary. She would settle for any human with a pulse. Slightly more discriminating ladies included the mother of Messalina's contemporary, the consul Curtius Rufus, who apparently resembled his father more than his mother's husband. The historian Tacitus admits to being embarrassed about the 'inglorious' circumstances of the conception. 'Many call him a gladiator's son. I don't want to lie about this, but telling the truth is a bit indelicate.'

The current emperor Commodus is fascinated by gladiators, and many Romans believe that one does not have to look far to find the reason.

There's a story, and a credible one at that, that Commodus, the emperor's son and successor, is no son of his at all. They say he's the product of an affair. There's an even more lurid story going around in the poorer areas. Faustina, daughter of [the emperor Antoninus] Pius, and the wife of [the emperor] Marcus [Aurelius] saw some gladiators on parade and was totally smitten with lust for one of them. ... When her husband consulted soothsayers about what should be done, they advised that the gladiator be killed while Faustina was underneath him, and she should wash in his blood as it fell, and then immediately lie with her husband. This sorted out the passion issue, but Commodus was born a gladiator ...

HISTORIA AUGUSTA: LIFE OF MARCUS AURELIUS 19

Annia Galeria Faustina, wife of the former emperor Marcus Aurelius. A lady who – if scandal-mongers are to be believed – was a secret gladiator groupie whose fascination with the arena severely affected the development of her son, the present emperor Commodus.

While this particular story should be taken with a bucketful of salt, it typifies the popular concept that identifies gladiators with wild and unrestrained sexuality. (There is a bronze figurine that amusingly takes issue with this, and depicts a gladiator in combat with his own massively endowed penis, which is arching back to attack him.) Not only are gladiators seen as sex-symbols but their blood has strange powers. In the marriage ceremony, a bride's hair is parted by a spear (a strange custom which the Romans themselves have trouble explaining). However, the ritual is all the more powerful if the spear has been dipped in the blood of a dead gladiator, as this would make the wife cleave to her husband even as the spear has cloven to the blood of the gladiator.

When it comes to being rented out for sex, if the price is right then a gladiator is supposed to summon up the steel and go for it. The men themselves have little say in this objectification of their bodies and their wanton use as instruments of carnal lust. However, in general they are thoroughly in favour and regard this as a not inconsiderable perk of the job.

Pull the other one, it has bells on it… The close connection between gladiators and sex is mocked in this bronze tintinnabulum (set of chimes) from Naples.

✤ ✤ ✤

Celadus the Thracian, three times victor and three times crowned, who makes the girls sigh.

(CIL 4.4397)

Crescens the net-man who catches girls by night.

(CIL 4356)

GRAFFITI BY GLADIATORS IN POMPEII, BOASTING
OF SEXUAL PROWESS

✤ ✤ ✤

In his guide to love, the poet Ovid warns of starting an affair just before a big show at the games, presumably because a potential lover might pale in contrast to the studs in the arena. However, it's not just the fairer sex who make a connection between lust and gladiatorial bloodletting, for after the games the arches (*fornices*) outside the arena habituated by prostitutes see such a busy trade that they have given later ages the verb 'to fornicate'.

The life of many a gladiator is basically nothing but violence leavened with bouts of mindless sex. Still, the philosophically minded might consider taking a walk through any cemetery and note the number of tombstones left by loving wives in memory of senior gladiators who trained hard in the *ludus* from IX to V and then came home to dinner and the kids.

Like many a job, that of a gladiator is basically what you make of it.

ABOVE   *This mosaic from the baths of Caracalla shows a naked victor holding the palm of victory and wearing his laurel crown. He holds a formal crown, possibly of gold or silver, as a more lasting memento of the occasion.*

✢ ✢ ✢

Lucius Pompeius of Vienne, a retiarius. After winning nine crowns as victor, he was slain aged 25. His wife Optata raised this memorial to her husband with her own money.

FUNERARY INSCRIPTION FOR A FALLEN GLADIATOR
AT COLONIA NEMAUSUS, IN GAUL

✢ ✢ ✢

Lucius the gladiator scratched a graffito for his sweetheart Lydia on this piece of pottery in Britain. It has proven a truly enduring memorial.

Women gladiators

Women gladiators fall into two groups – hardened professionals and wannabe fighters. The glamour of the arena does not affect only the males of a Roman household. In the same verse in which he excoriates Eppia for running off with a gladiator, Juvenal is every bit as scathing about women who want to be gladiators themselves.

✣ ✣ ✣

*I don't have to tell you of the athlete's cloaks and wrestler's
embrocations these women use
We've all seen one of them whacking at the palus [practice post]
Stabbing it through with a sword, charging it with a shield, and
doing it all by the book…
Perhaps indeed, she nurses the ambition of taking her skills
into the arena for real?
You can't expect modesty from a woman in a helmet
Who repudiates her own gender and delights in feats of strength
(Yet she knows the joys of womanhood too well to want to be a man)*

✣ ✣ ✣

*Here's a woman who finds the flimsiest of summer gowns too hot
Whose delicate flesh is irritated by the lightest of silk lingerie
Yet look at the coarse wrappings on her haunches
As she pants and grunts through her prescribed exercises,
Head bowed by the weight of her helmet.
What a laugh when she lays down her weapons
And squats to use the can!*

JUVENAL SATIRES 6

✣ ✣ ✣

Although gladiators are ostensibly the lowest of the low, there is something about the spectacle of combat in the arena that makes even wealthy ⇝

equestrians and the children of senators want to try it. Repeated legislation is enacted by good emperors to keep men of this class out of the arena, but under bad emperors, even women get to have a go. For example, during the reign of Nero, probably in his games of AD 63:

✝ ✝ ✝

Women, not just of the equestrian order, but even of the senatorial class, appeared in a shockingly disgraceful exhibition as though they were the scum of society. Some appeared in the theatre…or killed wild beasts, or fought as gladiators. Some were compelled to do so bitterly against their will, but some did so willingly.

CASSIUS DIO *HISTORY* 61.17

✝ ✝ ✝

Though Juvenal would have us believe that every upper-class household harbours a closet Amazon or two, the truth is that female gladiators are a rare breed, vanishingly so among senatorial families, but also hard to find in the ranks of professional gladiators. Nevertheless, they do exist, and their appearance is a sure-fire crowd-puller at any spectacle, even though the matrons mutter under their breath about how scandalous it all is. Female fighters are contrary to the feminine nature as the Romans understand it, and that of course is what makes the female gladiator such a draw at the games. This is exactly the nature of a spectacle – to show people the bizarre, something totally different from their humdrum daily lives.

And make no mistake, professional female gladiators can swing a sword with the best of them. These are not variety acts, such as dwarf fighters or the *paegniarii*, those mock-gladiators who clown about between scene changes and whose main purpose is to serve up some light relief amid the general carnage. Instead, when women gladiators appear in the games, it is in the mid-to-late afternoon show, the time when the serious combats are staged.

Female gladiators come to fight in the arena in much the same way as their male counterparts, although since the reign of Hadrian it has been illegal for slaves or maidservants to be sold to *lanistae*, unless the seller can produce

Amazonia and Achillia give a whole new meaning to the phrase 'lady-killers'. This relief from Halicarnassus in Asia Minor shows the fighters bare-headed, but since most spectators would know the gladiators by their helmets, these have been included at the bottom of the sculpture.

a good reason for doing so. Nevertheless, evidently good reasons are sometimes found, for female gladiators have appeared in spectacles both in Rome and the provinces. Visitors to Ostia can read an inscription there by Hostilianus of the town council, who proudly claims the achievement of being Ostia's 'first to give [displays of] women at the sword'.

The emperor Augustus, who was as prudish about public morality as he was unrestrained with his own love affairs, tried to limit the number of gladiators by a decree in AD 11 which banned those under the age of 20 from the arena. This restriction was deemed too narrow, and the emperor Tiberius followed this up with another in AD 19 which broadened the restriction to include all women of the senatorial and equestrian classes, or in fact the family of anyone who was high enough in society to have the right to sit in the front seats of the arena.

If the intention was to discourage woman gladiators as a class, the legislation has not been a great success. Female gladiators, if not common, are certainly widespread. For example, in Asia Minor one can see the bas-relief the people of Halicarnassus constructed in honour of two of their gladiatrices, Amazonia and Achillia, who fought so well that they both received the *missio*, or a reprieve from the arena (see p. 65).

Even the emperor Domitian (AD 81–96) enjoyed watching female gladiators in action. His biographer Suetonius tells us that he liked to stage fights by torchlight (which the gladiators certainly would not have enjoyed, because the flickering shadows make it harder to judge movement of a body or sword). Suetonius says that Domitian liked to match 'women and dwarves against each other', though it's hard to tell if he meant woman v. dwarf or dwarf v. dwarf and woman v. woman in separate bouts. It is unlikely to be the former, unless some kind of handicapping system was in operation, for a full-sized body, male or female, has great advantages in reach and strength.

It may well be that one of the major problems facing a female gladiator is simply that of finding a *ludus* prepared to take her on. *Lanistae* are Roman males after all, and are not immune to the sentiment of the day, which regards women fighting in the arena as an offence against nature and morality. There are also certain practical problems in adapting the all-male environment of a *ludus* to accommodate a female contingent, not to mention the mental adjustment required by the gladiators themselves. Apart from ratcheting the sexual tension in the establishment up another notch – and don't forget there are lots of other types of stress going on in these schools anyway – can you imagine the effect on morale if one of the woman gladiators proved better than the menfolk?

VII

Preliminaries to a Bout

When death happens daily before your eyes, you learn never to be greedy.

HANDBOOK OF EPICTETUS THE STOIC 21

✛ ✛ ✛

When combats take place

It's a common misconception that gladiatorial combats take place at the Roman games, those public festivities paid for in large part by the state. The Roman games themselves, especially the *ludi scaenici*, are about athletics and art (though it's not hard to track down a good orgy during the Floralia celebrations of early May). Most festivals feature a few days of chariot racing (*ludi circenses*), which can be just as hair-raising and lethal for the participants, but gladiator combats do not usually feature on the programme. As far as the state is concerned, gladiator combats are private affairs, whether staged by a dutiful son in his father's memory (the usual excuse in the Republic) or as a gift to the people by a beneficent leader. In Rome, the right to stage large-scale gladiator games is jealously guarded by the emperor. Nevertheless, occasions for gladiators to keep up their combat-readiness are not hard to come by.

✛ ✛ ✛

Everyone was gossiping about a man called Demochares [of Plataea in Greece] who was putting on a display of gladiators. He was a man who moved in the top social circles, and with his wealth and generosity he laid on amusements for the populace as splendidly as his status merited.

PETRONIUS *SATYRICON* 4.13

✛ ✛ ✛

Drama at the racetrack. Only the chariot races at the Circus Maximus rival gladiator bouts in the popular imagination, and unlike gladiatorial contests, chariot races are part of most official festivals.

Saturnalia

The exception to non-gladiatorial festivals is the Saturnalia, that strange midwinter celebration which is marked by drinking, public licence, goodwill, gift giving and gladiators killing each other. Because it is the one time of the year when gladiators are practically certain to fight, most are somewhat ambivalent about the joyous season.

Private munera

Gladiators like to keep in form, and many are uneasily aware that a gladiator who only fights in December is probably lacking the edge required to ensure survival until January. So it's not unusual for gladiators to badger their *lanistae* to fix them up with extra bouts, preferably against lower-quality opposition. Games staged on the cheap (for less than 30,000 *sestertii*) are called *munera assiforana* (see p. 122). As will be seen, the *lanista* does not get much compensation if his gladiators are killed in such mini-spectacles, and therefore he has a great incentive to ensure that his men survive the experience. In fact, at such games it is customary to use blunted weapons.

Imperial games

The emperor may decide to tack gladiatorial games on to the beginning or end of an 'official' festival, generally under the pretext of another victory for Roman arms somewhere on the empire's far-flung borders. Should the emperor himself leave Rome, especially on a military campaign, games are almost certain to celebrate his return, either to commemorate a success, or to take people's minds off a failure.

In fact the emperor can decide to stage games whenever suits his political agenda, for the games invariably boost his popular standing. And every emperor wants to be as popular as possible, for – as both Nero and Domitian discovered – an unpopular emperor might envy a gladiator his longer life expectancy.

Before the gladiators. This frieze depicts the various types of professional events (running, wrestling, discus) that traditionally make up the athletic events at a Roman festival. Gladiatorial games may be added as a climactic (but technically separate) event.

✛ ✛ ✛

The people, who once decided who would receive the top magistracies, command of the legions and everything else, now hold themselves back in the anxious expectation of receiving two things – bread and circuses.

JUVENAL *SATIRES* 10, 77 FF

✛ ✛ ✛

The imperial cult

Outside Rome, the priests of the imperial cult are among the major employers of gladiators. They are expected to provide games in the emperor's name, and to make them as generous as possible, since poor games reflect badly on both the individual presenting the games and on his opinion of the emperor.

The Roman games

A favourite time for gladiator combats coincides with the *ludi romani*, the Roman games that run from early to mid-September. There's always been a somewhat martial flavour to these games. In the early days of Rome, a general in a tight corner on the battlefield, or one setting off to campaign against unfavourable odds, would offer to hold games in honour of whatever god brought him victory. September is a month before the Armilustrium, the official end of the campaigning season. Nevertheless, this was often the time that a successful general returned to the city with a horde of prisoners, and a head full of ingenious ideas for spilling their blood in entertaining ways that would persuade the people to vote for him in the forthcoming elections. The tradition has continued into the imperial era, with pretexts often being found for a bit of gladiatorial blood to flow alongside the official festival.

Preliminaries to a fight

Cost of the event

✛ ✛ ✛

Lanistae should be warned that they do not have a licence for their immoral desire to profiteer…

DECREE OF THE EMPEROR MARCUS AURELIUS *CIL* 2.6278

✛ ✛ ✛

Naturally, once it has been decided to stage gladiator games, the very upper-class organizers do not deal directly with disreputable individuals (*infames*) such as the *lanista*. Instead, go-betweens make their way from senatorial houses to the gladiator school, and well before the games are publicly

*Lions, tigers and bears…*Venatores *take on a variety of beasts in this drawing of a 1st-century relief. Note the open-faced helmets and elaborately customized shields of the human participants.*

announced, negotiations are far advanced as to how many gladiators will be paired off to fight, and probably some rough agreement has been reached as to how many of these gladiators can be expected to perish.

This is important, as gladiators are just one aspect of the games for the organizers, who also have to arrange for animal hunts of beasts as wild and exotic as possible, ingeniously sadistic executions for criminals, the provision of musicians, dancers, acrobats, *sportulae* (gifts flung into the crowd), and payment for all of the above. For gladiators this includes an imperial tax of over 20 per cent that the *lanista* has to cover from his fee, which is known as the *praecipuum mercedis*. The *lanista* is also expected to pay his gladiators a share of this fee – even a slave should get about 20 per cent of his rental. How much the free *auctoratus* gets depends on how well he negotiated when he signed up.

In the provinces, a priest of the emperor can cut down expenses by owning the gladiatorial *familia* that takes part in the imperial games, and then regaining his expenses by letting the gladiators out for bouts elsewhere and then selling the whole lot to his successor when he leaves office.

It is important to manage expectations as to what kind of games are being offered to the public, as a crowd might give an enthusiastic response to a well-presented event of which they had modest expectations, yet boo the same games if they had been trumpeted as a once-in-a-lifetime experience. So games themselves are divided into four categories. The basic premise here is that the more money spent, the better the show will be. So we have the relatively cheap *munera assiforana*, which are basic run-of-the-mill affairs, good enough for a small- to medium-sized provincial town, but which the average citizen of Rome itself would hardly consider worth his while to see. Above this, ranked in ascending order, are:

IV   Modest affairs of up to 60,000 *sestertii*
III   Slap-up entertainments of up to 100,000 *sestertii*
II   Magnificent shows of up to 150,000 *sestertii*
I   All-out, no-expenses-spared bank-busting spectaculars of 200,000 *sestertii* or above

(As a rough guide, 15,000 *sestertii* represents about a lifetime's wages for a semi-skilled workman.)

Value of gladiators

Since we are talking figures, two numbers dominate the life of a gladiator – *tempus et pretium*, his time and his price. No one, the philosophers will tell you, can put a value on a human life or tell how long it will last. A *lanista* might beg to disagree. Most gladiators sign on for four or five years or the rest of their lives, depending which is shorter, and a good *lanista* can usually cut the lifetimes of his gladiators to suit his circumstances.

As to the price of a gladiator's life, the clerks have this figured to the last *sestertius*. This is because the organizers pay the *lanista* for every gladiator killed in combat. The pricing was fixed in an imperial decree of AD 177, and the table looks like this:

Value of games (in sestertii)

	IV	III	II	I
Dead Gladiator				
Class 1				15,000
Class 2			12,000	12,000
Class 3			10,000	9,000
Class 4		8,000	8,000	7,000
Class 5		6,000	6,000	6,000
Class 6	5,000	5,000	5,000	
Class 7	4,000			
Class 8	3,000			

So a first-class gladiator killed at a top-of-the-range event costs the organizers 15,000 *sestertii*, and a bottom-ranking gladiator at a minor spectacle costs 3,000. Note that the values given here are maxima – if the organizers can get the gladiators killed for less it's up to them to try to beat the *lanista* down. If he won't budge, the organizers might insist instead that gladiators fight more than one bout apiece during the games. 1,000 *sestertii* represents the top value of a *gregarius*, one of those semi-skilled gladiators who fight in groups. *Gregarii* are often prisoners of war, and as such fighters need little to no training, they can be disposed of at a profit even for this low price.

On the other hand, a gladiator who has survived three-and-a-half years is pretty good at his trade, and therefore high-ranking, and worth a lot of money if he is killed in a fight. Yet that same gladiator may be about to retire from the *ludus* and the profession, taking all that value with him. It does not take a genius to understand that such a person is worth more to the *lanista* dead in combat than alive and retired. Even most gladiators have figured it out. So a senior gladiator nearing retirement should take a very serious interest in exactly how final his final fights are intended to be.

If the organizers want to include a *libertus*, a gladiator who has made it to retirement, but who can pull in the crowds with his fame, then when it comes to bribing him to return to the arena, the sky is the limit.

Once the figures have been negotiated, the money is placed on deposit with a banker. Because gladiators are hired on what is essentially a 'you break them, you buy them' basis, most organizers try to limit their expenses by making sure that they have the best doctors on hand to restore life to wounded gladiators and their own endangered bank accounts. Organizers might also insist on the fights being stopped at the first sign of injury. For the gladiators in question, such deep concern for their well-being is highly reassuring, no matter what the motive.

Value of a ticket

Much depends on the motive of the person laying on the games:

Speculators are frankly out to make a profit. Such men will actually buy condemned criminals from the courts in order to kill them with spectacular flamboyance during the show. They carefully work out exactly how much stab per *sestertius* each gladiator is worth, and price their seats accordingly.

Imperial priests are staging the games as part of their role, but presenting even modest games represents a serious financial blow to the bank account of an average provincial aristocrat. So here too the organizer will be looking to charge as much for admission to the games as he can get away with.

Those seeking election to public office want to demonstrate their open-handed generosity, and are likely to heavily subsidize the cost of admission, or indeed remit it altogether.

Emperors are particularly prone to such generosity, because although they have already gained the highest office possible, they are understandably keen on living to enjoy it, and public support is essential for this.

However, just because an emperor or aspiring magistrate has handed out free tickets for the games, spectators will not necessarily get in for nothing. There are a lot more people in a town than seats in an arena, so what later economists will call a 'secondary market' quickly develops, with tickets being traded for cash or favours. If the coming games look spectacular, this market quickly becomes feverish.

The aediles *(city magistrates) of Pompeii announce that a* familia *of gladiators will be fighting in the arena. A* venatio *(animal hunt) is also scheduled. Et velae erunt means 'there will be awnings' – spectators will be shaded from the sun.*

A·SSVETTII·C ERII
AEDILIS·FAMILIA·GLADIATORIA·PVGNABIT
POMPEIS·PR·K·IVNIAS ·VENATIO·ET VELA·
ERVNT

Advertising

Whatever their motives for staging the games, the organizers want a good turn-out of spectators, so they hire publicists to bring word of the event to the public. This is done in various ways.

By word of mouth – announcements by criers at other theatrical or sporting events or even in the forum.

Posters called *libelli* are produced, giving the schedule of the event. Nailed up in taverns and market places, these rapidly collect a small crowd in which the literate members explain to their less fortunate fellows exactly what delights the organizers have in store.

Sign writers are hired to paint the programme on as public a wall as they can find, announcing in great detail who is scheduled to do what to whom.

Fight club

Marcus Maesonius presents his first gladiatorial show on May the second.

✠ ✠ ✠

There will be Thracian against Murmillo, [one] from the Neronian School, and twice a victor, against Tigris, [a gladiator] of the Neronian School, once a victor. [Another] of the Neronian School, three times a victor and once given a missio while still standing [i.e. the fight was called off] taking on Speculator, the victor of 69 combats. There will be Hoplomachus against Murmillo…

GLADIATOR PROGRAMME FROM POMPEII. *CIL* 4.2508
(THE LIST GOES ON TO DESCRIBE ABOUT A DOZEN
FORTHCOMING FIGHTS)

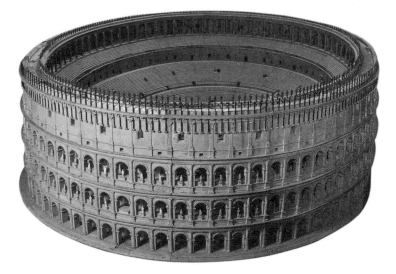

The Flavian Amphitheatre, as seen from the Esquiline Hill in Rome. This is the ultimate fighting arena, so close to the gladiatorial schools that the fighters can enter the amphitheatre through custom-built tunnels.

The venue

Almost anywhere one finds Romans one can find gladiator fights at some time or another. But by AD 180, all arenas everywhere are basically imitations of the one where every gladiator imagines himself fighting – in the greatest venue on earth, arguably the most bloodstained patch of ground anywhere on the planet: the Flavian Amphitheatrum, the Colosseum of Rome.

✛ ✛ ✛

Memphis shall speak no more of her wondrous pyramids, nor Assyria boast of Babylon…the Carians shall no more exalt their Mausoleum to the empty air of the skies. All yield before Caesar's Amphitheatre, the one work that replaces the fame of all.

MARTIAL ON *THE SPECTACLES* BK I

✛ ✛ ✛

Actually, this massive, awe-inspiring building itself is not called the Colosseum. The Flavian Amphitheatre (to name it properly) is in the Colosseum, which refers to the entire area in the valley between the Caelian and Esquiline Hills. The colossus after which the place is named is the massive bronze statue of the sun-god Helios which stands beside what most Romans simply call 'The Amphitheatre'.

Over 120 feet tall, the colossus is one of the few remaining relics of Nero's splendid Golden House. Like the Golden House itself, this is a massive monument to the narcissistic self-indulgence of the tyrant emperor, whom the statue was originally meant to depict. Once Nero was dead, his successor, the pragmatic Vespasian, demolished the entire building to 'give Rome back to itself' and built his amphitheatre where once a scenic lake had been. 'Nero' the statue was given a hasty makeover, and became 'Helios' the sun god, though there are rumours that Commodus intends a third identity change to make it 'Commodus the Gladiator'.

✢ ✢ ✢

There was a lake that seemed to be the size of a small sea, fringed with buildings as large as cities, and on the other side were vineyards, woods and pastures stocked with all sorts of domestic and wild animals.

SUETONIUS *LIFE OF NERO* 31
(DESCRIBING NERO'S BUCOLIC FANTASY, WHICH
THE COLOSSEUM REPLACED)

✢ ✢ ✢

However impressive the rest of Nero's Golden House may have been, it can only have paled into insignificance before the towering majesty of the building that has replaced it. Even 2,000 years later, this will be one of the most immediately identifiable buildings in the world, an iconic symbol of the might of Rome.

A gladiator who fights at the Colosseum is usually a denizen of the imperial *ludus* next door, and the looming mass of the amphitheatre is a part of the backdrop to his daily life. But step out of the *ludus* for a moment, and – standing perhaps in the cooling spray of the Meta Sudans, the ornamental fountain that is another landmark of the area – regard the amphitheatre as it must appear to someone seeing it for the first time.

At this distance, it is not so much a building as a multi-tiered curving cliff of stone. The stone is travertine, almost the colour of pale honey in the summer sun. You have to tip your head back to see the topmost tier 160 feet above, where banners attached to poles whip colourfully against the blue Roman sky. Painted shields (called *clipea*) hang between the windows of this topmost level, while below are three layers of deep-shadowed arches, each in a different order of classical architecture. Doric is on the ground level, Ionic on the next, and Corinthian on the third.

The arches make a circuit of 80 colonnades on each level, with those on the ground level serving as gates. Each gate is marked with a number corresponding to the ticket that those wanting to enter the amphitheatre to see a spectacle must present for inspection. Colourful bas-reliefs cover the arches.

As you wander around the building, its sheer bulk becomes ever more apparent. This one building is the size of a city block, 650 feet across at its longest and covering 6 acres of land. While appearing to have made their masterpiece entirely of stone, the builders have made lavish use of concrete in the inner corridors, hiding this beneath red-and-white paint or facings of marble.

The Flavian Amphitheatre so impressed one man that he had this contemporary snapshot carved on his tomb.

‑ ‑ ‑ ‑ ‑ ‑ ‑ ‑ ‑ ‑ ‑ ‑ ‑

Paving stones of travertine stone surround the building itself, with places where hurdles can be fitted to channel the crowds on the day of a spectacle. Here at the Meta Sudans fountain you are at a busy intersection, where four of Rome's administrative regions border each other. It's easy to pick out the city-dwellers, who hurry about their daily business and barely glance at one of the great architectural glories of the world. Tourists, perhaps in town for the festival, and possessing a prized ticket for the emperor's accompanying gladiatorial games, are equally easy to spot. Many come here to work out beforehand their best line of approach to the particular gate leading to their seat. (When tens of thousands of people are converging on the amphitheatre in a hurry is not the moment to discover you should be on the other side of the building.) Yet having come to reconnoitre, many remain to stand and wonder.

A building of such splendour, built at huge expense over almost a decade, has just one purpose – that men and animals should fight and die within, and the sight of their blood and pain should be displayed as intimately as possible to the spectators who crowd the artfully arranged seats. No wonder that, in a later, gentler age, a writer will behold this magnificent edifice and say:

✜　✜　✜

The gigantic Coliseum…must move all who look on it now, a ruin,
God be thanked, a ruin!

CHARLES DICKENS *PICTURES FROM ITALY*

✜　✜　✜

The people of the arena

Gladiators are the stars of the Colosseum, but they are a small part of a community that lives for and on the games. For every gladiator there are dozens of animal trainers, seamstresses, ticket touts, carpenters, scene shifters, jugglers, acrobats, decorators, musicians, tip-collectors and general workmen who form a tightly knit society with its own jargon, customs and priorities.

Most of these make the arena their career, and regard gladiators as ephemeral figures who are here today, dead tomorrow. They have seen dozens, if not hundreds, like you before. They are the people who will prepare your armour and the pomp and ceremony of your entrance, and may afterward carry your body from the arena, strip off the armour and wash it down for burial. Best to get to know them.

Taking part in the games as a gladiator for the first time is confusing and frightening enough already. When the games take place it's a very good idea to have already been behind the scenes and be familiar with what's going on. Inevitably, what the spectators see as a smoothly synchronized performance may look totally different to those behind the scenes. Right from the opening parade, when (for example) the lead trumpeter has gone unaccountably missing, one of the elephants has developed stage fright and a gladiator has taken violent exception to some decorative element of his costume, a performance of the games is guaranteed to turn the organizers into nervous wrecks.

A diagram showing part of the array of ropes and stanchions required to keep the awnings over the spectators during a performance.

Given the huge complexity of some of the special effects, and the general (in)efficiency of contemporary technology, it can be taken for granted that something mechanical will go wrong. Perhaps the huge awnings that protect spectators from the sun will get jammed (these awnings are so complex that they are operated by a special detachment of sailors from the fleet at Misenum stationed at the imperial *ludi* next door – see p. 133). The floor of the arena lies over a complex warren of storerooms, corridors and cages packed with victims (human and animal) of the forth-coming day's entertainment. The place is a shadowy maze of counterweights, ramps and winches, lit by lamps and torches and, on games days, filled with noise and highly stressed creatures – staff and 'performers' alike.

It might be that one of the cages containing a tiger will fail to open once the lifts have brought it to the surface, or even more catastrophically, open prematurely while still underground. The cable carrying a mock Icarus high over the amphitheatre might snap, sending the person it is carrying plummeting to earth in an all-too-faithful imitation of the original.

A giraffe is mistakenly released through a hidden trapdoor. This brings no complaints from the condemned criminals in the arena, who were expecting lions.

Such is the potential for disaster that the organizers know with sickening certainty that something will go wrong. They just don't know what it will be, when it will be, or how bad it will be. So, sometimes, when spectators see a gladiator standing bewildered after he has been hastily thrust out into the sunshine, this might be because the preceding act was cancelled for whatever reason. Now this poor fellow, who was counting on a quiet half-hour to compose himself before combat, has been hauled from his contemplative sojourn on the latrine, had his armour hastily buckled on, his helmet slapped on his head and has been told he will be fighting for his life in two minutes. On games days, it's best to expect the unexpected.

It's even better to stay ahead of events by cultivating friendships among the employees of the amphitheatre. The person who prepares your armour will do a better job if he feels he is doing it for a friend, and the musicians can help to influence the mood of the crowd. You'll get advance notice of any significant developments (such as that the emperor is feeling tetchy this afternoon) and thus a slight advantage over your opponent, who probably won't have made the same effort. (Gladiators are not usually people persons by inclination.)

VIII

Death at the Colosseum

You are not injured until you think you are injured.

HANDBOOK OF EPICTETUS THE STOIC 30

✛ ✛ ✛

In the imperial *ludi*

✛ ✛ ✛

We live our lives in the gladiatorial barracks, we fight against men with whom we share a drink.

SENECA ON ANGER 2.8.2

✛ ✛ ✛

The *procuratores* who supervise the imperial *ludi* are among the first to know when the emperor is planning a spectacular. Queries will have come down from the officials on the nearby Palatine Hill, asking how many gladiators are available and what condition they are in. It does not take long for news of this development to percolate through the entire complex, and suddenly training, always done with considerable intensity, acquires extra urgency. The imperial *ludi* cover a large area, but even this suddenly becomes claustrophobic as potential rivals assess each other, and each gladiator becomes aware that the person sitting next to him at table might soon be trying to carve him up as enthusiastically as he is now attacking his steak.

During practice sessions, trainers and senior gladiators stand together muttering and watching beady-eyed as tiros and lower-grade gladiators go through their paces. Long before the first handbills are written up, the *lanista* and the *doctores* will have lists of possible pairings. An entertaining fight will be as much about matching personalities as skill sets. Celer and Flamma loathe each other? Well and good, let the pair take their animosity out on to the sand and one way or another rid the *familia* of their brawling and squabbling. And the cool-headed Marcus Glauco will make an interesting counterpoint to the more skilful Proximo, who fights well – until his temper gets the better of him.

There is always rivalry among the different parts of the imperial *ludi*, but in the lead-up to a show this becomes potentially explosive. Before a fight is a good time to try to intimidate an opponent, and the more aggressive type of gladiator might well try to stage an 'accidental' confrontation with a potential rival to make sure that his psychological dominance is established before the two meet in the arena. Well before a fight, a wise administrator will keep a close eye on the interaction between the different parts of the gladiator complex.

The Ludus Matutinus Situated next to the Colosseum, the 'morning school' is partly outside the general rivalry, because, as the name suggests, its performers take part in the morning shows. They are the beast-hunters, and while there might be internal stresses and a severe disagreement about who gets to face a newly arrived batch of panthers, the fighters will at least all be on the same side come the big day. Also, they can't be happy that their craft is somehow considered inferior to that of 'real' gladiators, and are united in their resentment.

The Ludus Dacius is where the Thracian-style gladiators train. The school gets its name from the Dacians, a doughty nation of warriors from the mountains beyond the Danube, but it deals with most of the eastern styles of fighters. It is situated on the Oppian Hill, conveniently close to the baths of Trajan, and next to the large barrack block which houses the sailors from Misenum who operate the Amphitheatre's sunshades.

The Ludus Gallicus specializes in the *murmillo* style of gladiators, who evolved from the Gallic gladiators of the Republic. This *ludus* is the smallest of the schools, and there is no love lost between its members and those of the Ludus Dacius, against whom the school's members are often paired.

The Ludus Magnus is right next to the Ludus Matutinus, so close to the Amphitheatre that it is linked to it by an underground tunnel. This *ludus*, like the others, consists of a closed quadrangle of buildings for storage, administration and residence. There is a central training area with a limited amount of seating from which trainers and favoured guests can watch the gladiators at practice. The mock arena of the Ludus Magnus is larger than the others, and is used for training by those with specialized equipment such as the *essedari* (chariot fighters) and the cavalry-style *equites*. In fact the mini-amphitheatre here can seat 3,000, and is capable of hosting a small *munus* all by itself. Because some of the fighters in the Ludus Magnus will be killing each other on show day, tensions here run particularly high.

There are a number of specialized buildings nearby in the gladiator complex, including the **Summum Choragium** where scenery and machinery are stored. There's the armoury, since the authorities very sensibly keep gladiators and swords well apart except on officially sanctioned occasions. Every gladiator will at some point end up in the **Saniarum**, since this hospital treats not only fight-day wounds, but also everyday illnesses as well as bumps and breaks incurred during training. However, only one visit – at most – is required to the **Spoliarum**, where a dead gladiator is stripped of his armour and prepared for burial.

Once a gladiator knows who his actual opponent will be, there are several steps he should take.

Know your enemy

✢ ✢ ✢

Cassius concentrated entirely on the war, as a gladiator focuses on his opponent.

APPIAN *THE CIVIL WARS* 4.133

✢ ✢ ✢

The public handbills give the basic details of a gladiator – his name, type of weaponry, and the number of victories. As his opponent, you need to know much, much more. So talking to those who have sparred against him is essential. If he is in a different school, then you can assume that your *doctor* is on your side. He may even have seen your future antagonist fight, and will have a number of tips.

Temperament   Does this fighter play a long game, going for victory through debilitating cuts and flesh wounds, while giving his opponent minimal opportunity to retaliate, or does he go for a quick, high-risk closure that means one of you will end up stabbed through the heart within a minute?

Tricks   Are there any techniques that this gladiator favours, such as a sword beat-down (whacking the top edge of an opponent's sword so hard that the weapon temporarily points to the ground), followed by a body-charge and trip? Learn all your opponent's best moves by heart and spend a lot of time practising the counters, and make sure that you do your practising as privately as life in a busy *ludus* allows.

Turns   If a *murmillo* loses sight of someone who has slipped behind him, or a *retiarius* turns to avoid an onrushing *secutor*, will he turn to his right or his left? Usually a left-handed person looking behind or turning his body will turn anti-clockwise, and a right-handed person will turn clockwise. However, a gladiator might have trained himself to respond differently, depending on which leg is forward or whether he wants to bring his shield or sword into play as he turns.

Tells   Every fighter has these 'give aways'. It might be a slight tilt of the head or a scrape of the foot before a rush or a dip of the shoulder that happens before a real stab, but not with a feint. Obvious tells, such as pulling back the arm before a stab, are eliminated early in training (or the people with such tells are eliminated early in combat), but this still leaves small involuntary gestures which are very hard to avoid making. This is because constant practice allows a gladiator to act and respond at an instinctive level using pure muscle memory – so the tell is built into a series of movements that have become a conditioned reflex. And it's not easy to stop a reflex.

✢ ✢ ✢

To the gladiator on the sand, a facial expression, a twist of the hand, or a particular posture of the body warns of an adversary's intentions.

SENECA *LETTERS* 22.1

✢ ✢ ✢

Intimidate your opponent

The battle for mental dominance begins for some gladiators the moment they step into the *ludus* for the first time. Some people just have to be top dog, and this is how every good gladiator sees himself. So there's a lot of snarling, bullying and dominance displays even during everyday life. A gladiator who is accustomed to deferring to another in the *ludus* has that much more to do if he is going to defeat that same man in the arena.

Expect aggression from your opponent before the coming contest. He will take every opportunity to violently denigrate your skills and pass messages explaining in colourful detail exactly what he intends to do when he gets you out on the sand. Of course, it's a game that two can play, and the winner is the one who has a fearful, demoralized opponent who comes out expecting to lose. Play hard.

Know your odds

The authorities frown on gambling on the outcome of a fight, not least because this can lead to a certain degree of fixing of that outcome. This is commoner in smaller arenas where the loser is likely to survive. The Roman crowd will have no mercy on anyone they suspect of throwing a fight and if they feel strongly the emperor will probably defer to their wishes. It's harder to get someone to lose deliberately if they won't survive losing, but those who lose their bets love to cry 'foul'.

Despite official disapproval of gambling, human nature ensures there's always a lively 'book' going on the odds for a particular fight. No one knows you or your opponent better than you do, so if you like the odds being offered on your fight, get an agent to place a substantial bet on your behalf. Bet on yourself to win. If you lose, a gambling debt will be the least of your worries.

A practice bout. This is on gravel, so both gladiators fight wearing light boots. In the arena itself, sand would get into the boots and rapidly progress from an annoyance to a possibly fatal distraction.

ABOVE *A Thracian, with his distinctive curved sword and griffin helmet, clashes with a* provocator *on the sands of the arena. Note that the Thracian, though usually the more mobile of the pair, has chosen to fight with both legs protected.*

RIGHT *A* murmillo *drops on to one knee for a breather. The swords that these athletes wield weigh several pounds, and even the over-muscled arms of a gladiator soon feel the strain.*

OPPOSITE *Rufus the* hoplomachus *makes a charge. This 'Greek-style' fighter's gear and fighting technique are as far from that of the original Greek hoplite as the* retiarius *is from the fisherman he supposedly represents.*

Abandon hope, all you who enter here. A murmillo *stands guard at the entrance to the arena in Puetoli. Gladiators are also sometimes hired to cause grievous bodily harm outside the arena, if someone of influence requires it.*

- - - - - - -

RIGHT *Medusa the* provocatorix *prepares for combat, gently tapping the flat of her sword against her lavishly ornamented shield. Anonymous in her helmet, she relies on the shield to identify her to her fans in the audience.*

- - - - - - - - -

While those in the imperial ludi *perform in the Flavian Amphitheatre, others working the country circuits find a smaller audience in impromptu arenas constructed outside the town walls.*

RIGHT *Charun finishes off a mortally wounded man. Generally, a dying gladiator is hospitalized and treated with care. However, a violent criminal sentenced to die by the sword merits no such consideration.*

LEFT *Audax the* secutor *poses menacingly, his chest smeared with (someone else's) blood. One wonders whether the small tridents decorating his shield each denote a fallen* retiarius *opponent.*

BELOW *A murmillo duel, before a fascinated audience. Cognoscenti among the spectators debate technical points of the duel, such as whether the armoured* manica *is superior to the more flexible padded version.*

ABOVE *The stands are packed as* retiarus *squares off against* secutor. *Note the* secutor's *wide belt, which both provides support and protects the intestines and lower spine. His shield is of a quality the average legionary can only dream about.*

RIGHT *The* summa rudis *watches intently as these two gladiators clash. If the fight has to be stopped for any reason, it is his job to step between the sharp swords and get two highly excited and very dangerous men off each other's throats.*

- - - - - - - - - - - - - -

LEFT *Alexander the* retiarius *prepares to meet a charging opponent. Note how the shoulder shield is turned for maximum protection, while the net slyly sweeps across the grass below the helmeted Thracian's field of view.*

BELOW *Women practise sparring. While they are not in gladiator gear, it is obvious that gladiator fever is not limited to the male gender. Even aristocratic ladies might occasionally practise a bit of swordplay in the comfort and privacy of home.*

The *cena libera*

✝ ✝ ✝

Let us eat and drink, for tomorrow we die.

ST PAUL *1 CORINTHIANS* 15.32

✝ ✝ ✝

The games evolved from a quasi-religious ceremony, and one result of this is that all the performers being 'sacrificed' are certain of one last good meal the night before. Though there is some local variance, this meal is supposed to be open to all whose lives may be lost in the morning. So gladiators take their places on the dining couches together with beast-fighters and condemned criminals. There's even the occasional Christian, who may well take the opportunity to enquire of everyone's plans for the afterlife.

Members of the public are allowed to come and view the spectacle at the *cena libera*, and they will take careful note of the conduct of the gladiators they will be watching tomorrow. As we have seen, money may change hands in consequence.

It's not a good idea to merrily shovel down food even for those so inclined. Bear in mind that the food is being presented by the person who is putting on the games. He wants to show that he can be lavishly generous. The *ludus*, on the other hand, puts nutritional value and quantity before quality of cuisine. So expect the food at the *cena libera* to be considerably richer than your metabolism usually copes with, and partake modestly. Going to fight for your life in front of tens of thousands of bloodthirsty, baying spectators is already a bowel-loosening experience. It doesn't need help from last night's dinner.

Confer with your trainer. The best food to select is wheat-based food-stuffs, since these burn off their energy slowly, and will still have some benefit to your system the following afternoon. Meat is good, but only in moderation. Some gladiators might prefer to eat foods that will, if their metabolism is cooperative, move briskly through their system overnight leaving their bowels empty by fight time, with less chance of becoming infected if those bowels have to be put back in afterwards.

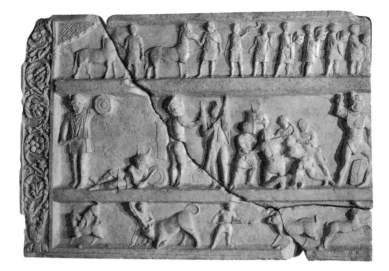

Others don't over-think it. 'It's free food, and good food, and perhaps the last I'll ever get. Time to pig out.' Such simple souls will probably finish the evening by flirting with anything female they can find, and probably get in a bit of mindless sex before sleeping soundly overnight. Envious gladiators who would like to murder these brutes for their insensitivity can console themselves that they will shortly get the opportunity.

There is more than a dinner going on here. For the condemned it's a last chance to say farewell to friends and family, and even gladiators take the chance to make a few arrangements with their loved ones, even if only to pass on instructions about what bets to place on whom.

✣ ✣ ✣

Even among the gladiators there are some who are not beasts. Like Greeks, they prefer to pass over gratifying their appetites with the lavish food in front of them, and instead take their pleasure in commending their wives to the care of their friends and setting free their slaves before they enter the arena.

PLUTARCH *MORALIA* 1099 B

✣ ✣ ✣

Games at Pompeii. The top of this bas-relief shows the pompa, *with musicians leading the parade. In the middle gladiators are in action – on the right, one gladiator has just scored a killing thrust under the ribs. In the beasts v. humans contests below, a bear finishes off a participant (right), and a bull is killed (left).*

- -

The march of the gladiators (*pompa*)

✛ ✛ ✛

The pompa comes first…the long line of [religious idols] the chairs
and chariots which carry them, the portable thrones and garlands…
so many sacred rites to observe, at the start, during, and at the end of the
procession. Priests and magistrates are called to march in the parade,
each known to the peoples of the city.

TERTULLIAN *ON THE SPECTACLES* 7.2–3

✛ ✛ ✛

The day of the games starts with the *pompa*. This is a procession into and around the arena: formal and magnificent enough to give the word 'pomp' to later generations. For those putting on the show, it's a nightmare to organize. For the gladiator it's a magnificent chance for self-advertisement, but also a chance to read the mood of the crowd and check out arrangements within the amphitheatre. For the spectators, the parade is an opportunity to see what is on offer over the coming days, and for the emperor, it's a chance to milk the applause of the public for the lavish spectacle he has laid on.

There's a certain order to these things. If the emperor is present – and if it's going to be a good show he probably will be – then the *pompa* should be led by his *lictores*. These men are the official escorts of any senior Roman official, and from time immemorial they have carried the *fasces*, that bundle of rods with an axe in the middle, which symbolizes the power of the state to chastise or execute. Traditionally within Rome the *fasces* are without their axe, but this does not mean that the emperor has no power to execute. There are several examples from history of emperors forcing stroppy spectators to get much more involved in the games than they would like.

Lictores *accompanying a magistrate outside Rome. We can tell this is outside the city, because each of the traditional bundles of rods contains an axe. Within city limits, magistrates have the power to flog wrong-doers, but the right to execute them is severely circumscribed.*

✛ ✛ ✛

[Caligula] once ordered that some of the crowd standing near the benches should be seized and thrown to the beasts; and to prevent the possibility of their publicly condemning his actions, he first had their tongues cut out.

CASSIUS DIO *HISTORY* 59.10

✛ ✛ ✛

Undoubtedly the organizers wish they could inflict a similar fate on some of those in the parade. It's easier when the *pompa* only has the gladiators on show, but that's not the case today. The gathering area near the Capitoline Hill is packed with tense participants already sweating gently in the morning heat. On this occasion there are elephants that have been trained to march in tandem. But the emperor is late, and no one is going to start the show without him. So the elephants are getting restless, and are shifting about and trumpeting, which is upsetting the tigers in their cages, and their snarls have upset the ostriches which are to be slain in an archery demonstration. Ostriches have a powerful kick, and the surgeons are already treating one victim.

Among the gladiators, Cassius is refusing to parade without his face-covering helmet, even though he protests to anyone who will listen that he is not an escaped slave. So the organizers have moved him into the second rank, which enrages him because he's the most hotly tipped newcomer of the year. Meanwhile Furius has discovered that the ornate but uncomfortable gilded armour he will be wearing in the *pompa* is the same armour he will have to wear while fighting, and he is, well, Furius.

There are acrobats fiddling with their costumes, a skimpily dressed dancer chasing a dwarf who has just given her an unwontedly intimate prod with his wooden sword, and an overall air of tension, stress and barely controlled adrenalin. Adrenalin levels jolt upwards once more as the *lictores* arrive. They brusquely shoulder their way through the dancers and acrobats on their way to the front (though they are noticeably more restrained about pushing through the crowd of edgy and armed gladiators). A roar from the amphitheatre announces that the emperor is now on his way to the *pulvinar* (the imperial box which naturally has the best view available of the arena, and gives the best possible view of the imperial person to his loving subjects). With the preliminary sacrifices and rituals and a blast of trumpets, the *pompa* gets underway.

The procession makes its way down through the forum, under the Arch of Titus and towards the Colosseum. The route is packed with those members of the public unable to get a seat in the amphitheatre. The gladiators come well back in the parade, preceded by the musicians, the images of the gods of Rome and their priests, and the animals, but all this just adds to the expectation of the crowd, and their cheers peak to a roar as you walk by. The gladiators preen, strut, show off outrageously and blow kisses to the maidens (or at least make bodily movements signifying extreme attraction). They won't get the chance to do this at the amphitheatre, since women are confined to the topmost, most distant tier (apart from the Vestal Virgins who sit in the front row, and who would certainly not take such gestures kindly).

There's an air of gaiety about the whole parade, reminding not a few of a festive Roman triumph for a returning army. Noisy as the crowd is along the way, as it cheers exotic animals or famed or notorious gladiators, nothing prepares the tiro for the sheer blast of sound that hits him as he enters the arena. About 50,000 close-packed spectators, most white-clad and waving their togas, bellow with enthusiasm. You know there is a water organ playing, because you can see the musician at work, but he is drowned by the general roar. Slaves appointed for the task use mini-catapults to lob little balls of wood into the crowd. There is a stir, and not a few punch-ups, wherever these small tokens land, for these *sportulae* are tokens for gifts from the presenter of the games, and possession of one is worth exchanging a few buffets to secure. The holder may find himself the proud owner of anything from a seaside mansion to a broken and empty eggshell. *In manibus Fortunae*, as they say.

A water organ and horn player from a mosaic in Germania. Musicians massage the mood of the crowd, and entertain them while the arena is prepared for the next event. The levers that operate the organ's pumps are just visible here.

✛ ✛ ✛

Little wooden balls with inscriptions for an item of food, or clothing, or vases or silver or gold, horses, pack animals or slaves. Those who seized the balls carried them to imperial officials who distributed the bounty.

CASSIUS DIO *HISTORY* 66.25

✛ ✛ ✛

Along with the rest of the parade, the gladiators stop to salute the imperial box, and the images of the gods that stand nearby. (Claudius used to have the images covered if things got too bloody.) Don't expect the ritual greeting favoured by the excited imagination of later generations. Only once have fighters said *Ave Caesar, morituri te salutant* ('Hail Caesar, those about to die salute you') and they were not proper gladiators and not in Rome.

As the procession circles the arena, take a look at the slaves carrying the tray on which the victory palms and prizes of silver are displayed, and also consider the Porta Libertinensis (the Gate of the Dead). Most of the gladiators in the procession will enjoy either the prize or a ride through the gate before the games are through. The parade wends its way back through the Porta Sanavivaria (the Gate of Life) and into the gloom of the tunnel where it breaks up in some confusion. The gladiators peel off and head back to their *ludi*, to relax, do a bit of light sparring and exercise, and maybe later enjoy a light lunch. They have a busy afternoon ahead.

Animal hunts once happened elsewhere in Rome. Events such as the one shown here at the Circus Maximus have given later generations the word 'circus' for displays involving acrobats, animals and clowns.

- - - - - - - -

The beast-hunt (*venatio*)

Beyond the huge metropolis of Rome lies the Italian countryside, where mothers worry lest their children gathering fruit or berries in the woods might disturb a bear, or encounter a stag in rut. And what traveller on a lonely country road has not tried with panicky hands to soothe a horse startled by wolf howls floating eerily through the gathering twilight? Yet terrifying as these beasts can be, the peoples of Italy know that compared to the lions of Africa, or the panthers and serpents of Asia Minor, their own wildlife is relatively benign. In part this explains the beast-hunt.

For the contemporary peoples of the Mediterranean, nature is not under threat, but ever-present and threatening. The beast-hunts of the games provide the reassuring spectacle of man asserting violent mastery over nature. Tell a Roman that the demand for panthers in the arena has almost wiped the species out in Asia Minor, and he will assume that you are complimenting the games, just as if you had noted that the games have caused a substantial reduction in the number of violent muggers in Rome. (And this is precisely why violent muggers get more or less the same treatment as the panthers.)

In fact the Romans use one menace to dispose of the other. Criminals are thrown to the beasts to kill or be killed. Sometimes, though, the morality is less defensible, for example when the organizer of the games takes the opportunity to dispose of any of his slaves who has displeased him.

✛ ✛ ✛

There's Glyco's steward, who was caught having it off with his mistress [Glyco's wife]. Well, in any crowd there are jealous husbands feuding with lover-boys. But Glyco having his steward thrown to the beasts, that's petty, as well as telling the whole world what's happened. He should have sent his old douche-bag in to be tossed by the bull – it's hardly the slave's fault when he has to obey orders. But then, if you can't beat the donkey, you'll hit the saddle.

PETRONIUS *SATYRICON* 45

✛ ✛ ✛

There are few rules about the form the 'beast-hunt' should take, apart from the general expectation that it should take place in the morning. That's partly because (to the bitter resentment of the beast-fighters) they would be an anti-climax if they followed the gladiators. It's also because animals kept in cages extremely close to creatures that they would flee from or fight in the wild tend very quickly to become exhausted by stress, so it's best to show them while they are at their most spirited.

The Roman crowd (which can include a large number of those devoted to their pets) cheer as happily when a bear is being ripped apart by a hunter as when a bear rips a condemned criminal to pieces. When it comes to bloodshed, the spectators are neither sensitive nor inclined to discriminate between species.

Animals can appear in a number of different roles:

Executioners

The Romans believe that justice should not merely be seen to be done, but done with such imaginative sadism as to make an indelible impression upon the imagination of potential wrong-doers. In a society without a police force, many Romans feel at the mercy of criminals. So when the sandal is on the other foot, little mercy is offered to criminals.

Criminals sentenced ad bestias in a North African mosaic. The audience considers that the bandits, rapists and murderers sentenced to this fate are themselves little better than wild beasts.

⁓ ⁓ ⁓

I saw Silurus [a bandit from southern Italy] torn to pieces by wild animals…he was put on a scaffold, above cages made deliberately fragile for this purpose. The scaffold was made to break and collapse, dropping him on to the cages.

STRABO *GEOGRAPHY* 6.2

⁓ ⁓ ⁓

Defenders of such barbarity argue that criminals must be removed from society, and if they are to be killed why not make a spectacle of it? Being killed by a lion is not in itself much worse than being hanged, and after death a corpse does not much care what happens to it. This may be a valid viewpoint, but it is harder to refute the later Christian argument that those degraded by the spectacle are not the messily deceased, but the spectators.

A woman tied to a bull is killed by a jungle cat in this terracotta relief.
Many female victims are 'poisoners' – a dubious charge, since Roman medical
forensics cannot always establish cause of death.

✠ ✠ ✠

Their greatest pleasure is making men die, or worse and more cruel, to have
them torn to bits. The bellies of wild beasts are engorged with human flesh,
which so delights the spectators that the victims are as much devoured by the
eyes of the audience as by the teeth of the animals.

SALVIAN *THE GOVERNMENT OF GOD* 6.2.10

✠ ✠ ✠

An Asiatic tiger fights a German wild boar. To the Romans this is not animal cruelty, but two dangers to human life and limb being forced to cancel each other out.

Beast-to-beast combats

+ + +

...I saw sea calves, with bears pitted against them.

CALPURNIUS SICULUS *ECLOGUES* 7.24

+ + +

...the rhinoceros blazing forth with terrible fury and lowered head. Such was the power of his double horn that the bear was tossed as a bull tosses dummies towards the stars!

MARTIAL ON *THE SPECTACLES* 26

+ + +

Again, apologists would argue that such spectacles show one killer pitted against another – a rhinoceros killing a bear in the arena means that both are not back in their native habitat killing humans. Still, it is hard not to feel a certain satisfaction on reading Pliny's report of animals massed for one such spectacle. These almost erupted through the barriers separating them from the audience. As Pliny remarks in deadpan Roman style, *non sine vexatione populi* – 'not without somewhat distressing the crowd'.

An elephant rider guides his mount to victory over a bull in this Roman mosaic from the Aventine Hill. Editores constantly seek new and entertaining contests for audiences bored by ordinary pain and bloodshed.

Against humans

✢ ✢ ✢

But one elephant did wonders, for when his feet were pierced with darts, he crawled upon his knees among his attackers, wrenched their shields from them and flung them aloft, and these turned and fell so neatly that it might have been contrived by an artist and not by a beast in its violent anger.

PLINY THE ELDER *NATURAL HISTORY* 8.7

✢ ✢ ✢

Even urban Romans see hunting as a way of gathering food, as the hares which appear in the weekly markets testify. So if there is such a thing as a typical arena beast-hunt, it is of exotic and savage creatures contending against humans – often volunteers armed and trained for the occasion – but it's a hunt nevertheless. And as with any hunt, the animals killed are promptly recycled into meat.

✢ ✢ ✢

He exhibited panthers, which were hunted down by horsemen.

SUETONIUS *LIFE OF CLAUDIUS* 21

✢ ✢ ✢

Butcher's shops happily sell off giraffe or hippopotamus fillets in the days following the games. In fact, after the first elephants were exhibited in Rome in 251 BC, the beasts were killed and eaten – probably because the Romans simply did not know what else to do with them. Very few animals are wholly discarded. Wealthy Romans have highly adventurous palates and are prepared to eat almost anything once, and the Roman poor are largely vegetarian simply because meat is an expensive luxury. When Caesar is providing free food, the plebs are more than happy to wolf down steaks, even if they are wolf steaks.

Still, as with any hunt, things do not always go to plan. In 55 BC Pompey arranged for elephants to be killed in the arena to boost his popularity with the crowd. However, he apparently selected domesticated animals, and the confusion and distress of these elephants when they were attacked so moved the spectators that the event ended with the spectators standing, waving their fists and shouting curses at Pompey.

Pornographic displays

The Golden Ass of Apuleius is a novel fated to be read for millennia hence. Its hero, Lucius, has been magically transformed into a donkey, and his owner has designs upon his body:

✛ ✛ ✛

He obtained a degraded creature whom the governor had condemned to the beasts. She was to prostitute herself with me in front of the crowd – as he believed that this was certain to get him a full house…a soldier came to fetch the woman who, as I said, had for her crimes been condemned to the beasts and was to partner me on our 'honeymoon'.

Already our marital bed was being lovingly made up, an affair of polished Indian tortoiseshell, piled high with brightly-covered cushions stuffed with goose feathers. Apart from the shame of having to do this act in public, and apart from degrading myself with this loathsome and detestable woman, I was in great fear for my life.

As I saw it, there we should be, locked together in a loving embrace, and whatever animal was let loose to devour the woman was hardly likely to be so discriminating, well-trained and firmly in control of its instincts that it would tear the woman to pieces and spare the innocent party – me!

APULEIUS *THE GOLDEN ASS*

✛ ✛ ✛

Such appalling occasions are not fiction, as is confirmed by the comment of Martial:

✛ ✛ ✛

Believe that Pasiphae made love to a Cretan bull – we have seen it.
The old story has been confirmed. Let not venerable antiquity boast of itself,
Caesar. Whatever fame celebrates, the arena reproduces for you.

MARTIAL ON *THE SPECTACLES* 5

✛ ✛ ✛

However, these 'performances' are relatively uncommon. So rare in fact, that souvenir shops may produce little oil lamps commemorating the sight in detail for those who don't want to get it out of their minds as fast as possible.

Other displays

Not all animals that enter the arena are dragged out on a butcher's hook. Even the Roman crowd gets tired of unrelenting bloodshed. So while new victims are being readied, non-lethal displays are presented to the crowd, such as bull-wrestlers, dancing elephants, or acrobats on horseback. Some really exotic animals can wow a crowd by their appearance alone.

✛ ✛ ✛

Furthermore, if any rare beast was worth seeing and it was brought to the
city when no games were taking place, he made it his habit to exhibit
them elsewhere. So a rhinoceros was displayed in the voting area on the
Campus Martius, a tiger on the stage, and a snake 75 feet in length in
front of the senate house.

SUETONIUS *LIFE OF AUGUSTUS* 43

✛ ✛ ✛

He built a kind of hunting-theatre of wood, which was called an
amphitheatre from the fact that it had seats all around without any stage.
In honour of this and of his daughter he exhibited combats of wild beasts
and gladiators…and here the so-called camelopard [giraffe] was introduced
into Rome by Caesar and exhibited to all.

CASSIUS DIO *HISTORY* 43.22 FF

Lunch break

Apart from gladiators, who are notorious for late nights and being somewhat sluggish in the early morning, Romans get up before cock-crow. It's not uncommon for an important Roman to have exercised, breakfasted, written a letter or two and seen his clients all before sunrise. These early mornings have to be paid for at some point, and that's usually midday, when the arena is a brightly lit circle of dazzling white sand spotlit by the sun, which makes coloured shadows dance and ripple among the seats of the amphitheatre as it is filtered by the filmy, gaudily coloured cloth of the awnings.

Because they have tickets, the spectators are happy to flock home, knowing that no one is going to nick their seats. 'Lunch' Roman-style is a lengthy business. If done properly it includes a light nap and (for those men who find the dances between the spectacles sufficiently suggestive) a cuddle with a slave girl.

As the seats empty, the pace of events in the arena slackens, though entertainment continues for the benefit of those die-hards who are not going anywhere. About the time that the tiro gladiator is contemplating whether he is up to a light salad, athletic displays or knock-about farces by clowns or performances by singers are taking place on the newly swept sand of the arena.

Sometimes a spectator dropping in for a bit of such light fare might find that the organizers have taken the opportunity of the lunch break to clear the books of unwanted criminals scheduled for disposal.

✛ ✛ ✛

The other day at midday, I happened to stop by at the games. I was expecting sport and something witty to rest the eye from the sight of human blood. It was the other way around. The morning combats were nothing. No one was messing about here – this was butchery plain and simple.

The men had no protection. They were completely open to every stab, and every stab was effective. The mob prefer this to balanced fights between selected pairs. And why not? The blade is not parried by helmet or shield, and defensive skill just delays death for a minute.

In the morning men are thrown to bears or lions, at midday they are thrown to the spectators. The crowd bays for killers to be matched against those who will kill them, and the winner is killed by someone else. There's no release or escape but death for these combatants, so they need fire and steel to drive them to fight. And the fights are always to the death…

Yes, he was a bandit, a murderer, and deserves what he gets – but what have you done, that you have to watch it? 'Kill him! [They shout] Whip him! Burn him alive! Why won't the coward rush on to the blade? Why does he try to avoid death?'

SENECA *LETTERS* 7

✣ ✣ ✣

This is another reason why the animal shows are staged in the morning. By the time the gladiators step on to the sand, the amphitheatre smells like what its critics claim it really is – an abattoir with pretensions. Even over the scent of the garlands decorating the arches, the tangy smell of take-away food from the vendors outside, and the overall aroma of sweaty Roman, the coppery, slightly cloying smell of blood hangs heavy enough in the air for human noses to smell. And if humans can detect it, imagine how it must affect the animals.

The opening bouts

The spectators start filtering back, refreshed by the break. The designers of the amphitheatre have planned well for the ebb and flow of this human tide. The wide stairwells and corridors that give easy access to exits are called *vomitoria*, which colourfully describes how quickly they can disgorge (or soak in) a crowd on the streets.

Right now, no one's leaving. There's a buzz in the air as those taking their seats contemplate the *libellus munerarius*, the programme for the afternoon. Not a few spirited arguments develop in the growing crowd about the merits of one gladiator or the other. Even the emperor in his imperial box may abandon his dignity to chaff with spectators about the prospects in a forthcoming fight. Famously, the emperor Domitian once got personally involved in such a discussion.

✣ ✣ ✣

He ordered that a man who remarked that a Thracian-style gladiator was
'a match for the murmillo, but not for the giver of the games' should be
dragged from his seat and thrown to the dogs in the arena while displaying
the placard 'An impertinent Thracian fan'.

SUETONIUS *LIFE OF DOMITIAN* 10

(THE THRACIAN FAN WAS IMPLYING THAT THE EMPEROR HAD
WEIGHTED THE ODDS AGAINST HIS MAN, PERHAPS OUT
OF DOMITIAN'S DISLIKE FOR HIS BROTHER TITUS, WHO HAD
FAVOURED THE THRACIANS)

✣ ✣ ✣

Sometimes partisanship can get completely out of hand, as happened at Pompeii a few generations ago. There the actual gladiators got to sit back and watch while members of the crowd ripped into each other with everything from fists to swords. The problem was with a large contingent of spectators at the games from the nearby rival town of Nuceria, with whom the Pompeians had irreconcilable differences. The Pompeians killed a large number of Nucerians and were punished by a decree forbidding them to hold any more gladiator shows for ten years. (After which the town was buried under volcanic ash, perhaps because Jupiter also disapproved.)

Today at the amphitheatre there's nothing stronger than light banter mingling with the oompah-pah of a tuba as a clown stages a carefully contrived pratfall. Such mock-fights among clowns are a way of whetting the returning crowd's appetite for the real thing. At this point there may also be exhibition matches by retired fighters. These old favourites use wooden swords, and demonstrate their skill and technique to the aficionados who are there to see true expertise with weapons just as the lunchtime spectators were there to see unmitigated bloodshed. There may also be a 'comic' display by *andabatae* – condemned criminals with gladiator training who fight either blindfolded under their helmets or with specially designed headgear. Unable to see their opponents, they are manoeuvred together by the attendants and slash blindly at their opponents. The bloodshed is real, and helps to get the spectators further worked up for the first of the proper gladiatorial combats.

Death of a gladiator

Put yourself in the sandals of Verus, a tiro *murmillo* gladiator facing his first bout in the imperial amphitheatre. This afternoon, his opponent will be a Thracian called Priscus. Priscus is a veteran, slave-born and sentenced to the arena for his savage temperament. He's feeling particularly savage today, because he sees being matched against a beginner as an insult. Yet the combat is not the mismatch it seems, for Priscus is coming back from a severe injury and, though he won his last fight (and the three before that), the muscles in his shoulder are newly healed. His trainers want to start him with an easy fight, and have decided you will be it.

So the mid-afternoon sees you in the *ludus*, sparring lightly with the *doctor*, who wears Thracian gear, and carefully takes you once again through some of Priscus's favourite routines. The amphitheatre next door has fallen quiet, and you know that the arena officials have entered.

The serious business begins. In the first bout of the afternoon a retiarius *squares off against a* secutor *as the* summa rudis *steps back.*

The *summa rudis* is the chief referee. Clad in a white tunic with two wide stripes down from the shoulder, he carries the stick which he separates the combatants if there's a break in the fighting. The *secunda rudis*, his second in command, is usually a pretty burly figure, because when their blood is up, not all gladiators stop fighting to order.

✜ ✜ ✜

He [Caligula] gave the signal for death to five retiarii who had put up a dismal showing against the secutores against whom they had been matched. At that, one of them seized a trident and killed each of his opponents in turn.

SUETONIUS *LIFE OF CALIGULA* 30

✜ ✜ ✜

Harenarii (sometimes called *libertinarii*), arena slaves, assist the two umpires and are also charged with cleaning up the arena after each bout. Nearby is the charcoal-filled brazier with the hot irons, which they have recently used to drive the condemned to fight each other. No true gladiator needs such incentive, but the irons will test for a flinch to see if a gladiator is dead or semi-conscious once taken down.

Hermes Psychopompus, the god who guides souls to the underworld (or at least an official dressed as such), stands by the Porta Libertinensis, ready to carry the deceased through the Gate of the Dead once they have fallen.

Charun, the demon, stands by with his mighty double-headed hammer to remove all doubt that those Hermes takes away are truly dead. Charun is of Etruscan origin, and even spectators sometimes confuse him with Charon, the ferryman of the Styx.

The first task of these officials is the presentation of the weapons, the *probatio armorum*. Here, the swords that the gladiators will use are shown to the *munerarius*, the giver of the games, so that he can personally ensure that the weapons are as sharp (or as blunt) as he has specified. One emperor used this occasion to shame a would-be conspirator.

✜ ✜ ✜

While Calpurnius Crassus…and some others who plotted against him [Nerva] were still ignorant of the fact that their plot had been revealed, the emperor invited them to sit beside him at a spectacle. When, as is generally the custom, he was presented with the swords to see if they were sharp he passed them to his guests, allegedly for them to check, but really to show that he did not care if he died then and there.

CASSIUS DIO *HISTORY* 68.3

For the tiro gladiator, warmed up and ready to fight, the delay before his bout cannot be easy. In fact, for those inexperienced in the ways of the amphitheatre it is all rather confusing. You are handed over to an official who, after a brief inspection, passes you to an attendant who evidently has several other matters on his mind.

Remember that the members of staff have processed hundreds of gladiators in their time. Trust them to know when you are supposed to enter, and how. It is probably at this point (procedures for these things are not fixed) that you get to handle the edged weapon you will be fighting with. Gladiators not in combat are usually kept away from anything sharp, on the same general principle that a naked flame is kept well away from oil. However, even arena officials have to accept that, to ensure a good fight, the protagonists have to be acquainted with the balance and heft of their weapon.

Everyone steps well clear as you execute a few practice moves and feints. The weapon feels very familiar – unsurprising since the person who prepared the blunted practice weapon based it on the real thing – but it is reassuring nevertheless.

Outside, in the amphitheatre, the excited shouts of the crowd give a measure of how the opening bout is going. The building's superb design means that despite the massive size of the crowd, the combat on the floor of the arena is strikingly intimate and immediate for every spectator, and even newcomers are pulled right in. One such, a young man called Alyptus, thought he was immune …

✛ ✛ ✛

… being utterly averse to and detesting such spectacles. One day by chance he met some acquaintances and fellow-students coming from dinner, and they hauled him, kicking and screaming, into the Amphitheatre during one of these cruel, deadly shows…the man he saw fall had taken a wound through the body, yet he himself was struck even more savagely in the soul…as soon as he saw that blood, he became drunk with the brutality of it all. He could not turn away, but remained staring, drinking in the frenzy, mindlessly delighted with that guilty fight, and intoxicated with the whole bloody pastime.

AUGUSTINE *CONFESSIONS* 6.8

✛ ✛ ✛

The spectators cry *habet!* ('he's taken one!'), and you know that one of the fighters is wounded. How badly becomes apparent from the brief silence, which indicates that the umpires have stopped the fight. Then the yelling begins again, ever louder, as the audience try to influence the emperor's decision as to whether the defeated gladiator should live or die. Shouts of *mitte* ('let him go') are slowly drowned by a chorus of *iugula! iugula!* ('kill! kill!'). Then there's silence as the emperor 'turns his thumb' (*pollice verso*).

✢   ✢   ✢

In the battles of gladiators…we are accustomed to dislike those who are timid and suppliant, and who beg for their lives, and we wish to save those who are brave and courageous, and who offer themselves cheerfully to death. We feel more pity for those who do not ask for it than we feel for those who plead for it.

CICERO *PRO MILONE* 34

✢   ✢   ✢

What's important here is not whether the thumb goes up or down, but what the gesture signifies. Thumbs down plus a vigorous stabbing motion may indicate that the thumb represents a sword stabbing the hapless loser. But thumbs up can mean the same if it is part of the same gesture that the emperor would use if he were personally stabbing down through the neck of the defeated gladiator. Ever a showman, the emperor milks the anticipation of the crowd, and then slowly reveals his decision to the defeated gladiator who stands before him, stoically ignoring the blood which pulses slowly from a deep wound under his ribs.

There's a different texture to the shout when the emperor's decision is revealed. This one has a hungry, anticipatory edge to it. You don't even have to glance at the emperor to know he has chosen death. You also know this is not pure sadism. Blood is welling out of the gladiator's wound in dark, thick gouts. The expert eye of the emperor has noted that the liver has been deeply penetrated, and possibly a kidney as well. Even with expert attention, the gladiator will probably perish, so the emperor might as well 'generously' sacrifice him to the crowd's bloodlust.

There's a ritual to what happens next. For the defeated gladiator, this is his last chance at redemption. He's going to die, but he can choose whether to be butchered like an animal, or, by voluntarily embracing his death, die like a free man.

✠ ✠ ✠

Consider gladiators…who are trained to receive a blow if it would be shameful to avoid it…which of them, even if run-of-the-mill average, lets out a groan when struck, or even changes his expression? Forget about disgracing themselves on their feet – they do not even shame themselves when they fall. Who, when defeated, tries to pull his neck away from the killing stroke?

CICERO *TUSCULAN DISPUTATIONS* 2.17

✠ ✠ ✠

This frieze comes from a Pompeii necropolis. In the centre, a gladiator steadies himself against his executioner's thigh as he kneels to await the killing stroke. At times like this a gladiator is glad that helmets hide the faces of all concerned.

There's a breathless silence as the wounded gladiator kneels. He sways slightly, and his opponent-turned-executioner lends a steadying hand. His victim firmly grasps the thigh of the man in front of him, and slowly bends his neck forwards. The executioner lifts his sword high, and because this is after all a spectacle, holds it there for the crowd to see. Then, to another roar from the spectators, he stabs down hard, sending the sharpened blade ripping through muscle, lungs and heart. It's a clean, practised kill.

You come to the entry gate as the corpse is loaded on to a stretcher to be carried off. Professionally, you note the bloodied sand being raked away and the fresh white sand sprinkled in its place. (Fresh sand over wet blood can get slippery if it is not deep enough.)

The victorious gladiator stands, taking in the applause of the crowd. His face is still hidden by his helmet, but small turns of the neck indicate that he is following the progress of attendants as they move through the crowd. The attendants hold silver collection trays, and collect tips from those who particularly enjoyed his performance. Since gladiators are notoriously vainglorious, he will treasure his palm of victory, and ensure it impresses and intimidates his barrack mates back in the *ludus*. But the real payoff is the cash prize, augmented by the tips now being collected.

There's a deliberate symbolism to the display. The victor reaps the spoils, standing in the light of the afternoon sun, sword raised high as the spectators clap and cheer. The loser, dead and disregarded, is almost forgotten by the crowd before his body has been swallowed up in the shadows of the Gate of the Dead.

An attendant taps you almost apologetically on the arm, and adrenalin surges through your body.

You're on.

A murmillo takes a breather as he contemplates his coming bout. He rests his shield against the padding on his left leg to take the strain off his shield arm. He has to hold his sword because, unlike a soldier, a gladiator has no sword belt or sheath. The only time a gladiator holds a sword is when he is about to use it in action.

- - - - - - - -

Out on the sand

Here's a tip. A gladiator's helmet hides his face completely, so forget that this is Priscus. Priscus is an ill-tempered boor, and you mildly dislike him, but that's not enough. You must hate, truly hate the man behind that helmet. So imagine he's the teacher who whipped you through your studies, gloating at your helplessness. He's the bully who victimized all the boys in your apartment block, the sneering aristocrat who filched your girlfriend, the debt-collector who terrorized your family and put you in the arena. He's all of these, rolled into one. You don't just want to kill him, you want to rip him into bloody giblets and jump on the bits. Still, if life in gladiator barracks has taught you anything, it's how to channel your anger. So you feel not uncontrolled (and therefore dangerous) fury, but a deep, burning hatred that's almost refreshing in its purity.

✢ ✢ ✢

With what energy he rushed out into the arena, enraged
against his opponent!

QUINTILIAN *DECLAMATIONS* 9

✢ ✢ ✢

The veterans say that the first time you face naked steel in earnest is an event you remember for the rest of your life. (Though the veterans also point out that this might not be much of a feat of memory.) Certainly, if your presentation to the crowd was something of a blur, and even your salute to the emperor somewhat vague in your mind, now the fight has started in earnest, everything has an almost unnatural clarity. A small part of you is aware of the crowd, but all your attention is on Priscus.

He advances quickly, confidently. He's evidently eager to finish things quickly. Perhaps that shield arm is still not ready for a prolonged bout? Advance to meet him, but move slightly towards his shield side, your own shield held slightly forward, and the sword hidden behind it. Now rush, clashing shield on shield, forcing him to strain that shoulder. Twist further behind your shield to avoid his stab, and spin out of contact, circling. An over-extended stab and you catch his forearm hard with the side of your shield. The arm is padded, but the impact throws him off-balance. Step in, stab hard underarm, and he leaps back, so you follow up with another shoulder-bruising shield charge.

He backs off, circling, and you turn to meet him, realizing too late he's turning you to get the sun in your eyes. Momentarily blinded, you rush forward, remember that Priscus likes to trip, and risk exposing your throat by bringing your shield down hard. There's a satisfactory jolt of shield edge on shin, and you both separate again, breathing hard. Priscus is limping a bit, but you are startled to feel blood trickling down your ribs. You don't even remember getting the cut.

He charges, and you smoothly counter and disengage, almost as if the pair of you were on the training floor. He tries to kick the bottom of your shield to hook down the top. It's an unexpectedly risky move for mortal combat, but you've been warned and are ready for it. Let the move happen and follow up by smashing your shield at his face, stepping forward and stabbing at the same time. Now it's he who disengages, but you've managed another good thump on his shield to strain his shoulder muscles.

Mosaic of gladiators in action from a villa in Rome. Note the Greek symbol 'theta' underneath the name of Astivus. This stands for Thanatos – Death.

The fight goes on, and it's clear to everyone that you are not out-matched. Stepping past his charge, you get in a backhand that scores a deep cut across his back, and both of you are dripping blood on to the sand as you square off again. Now he comes at you and it's a furious few moments of blocking, backing and counter-stabbing. So much is done by instinct that at

In the centre of this mosaic a murmillo *turns to raise his finger in appeal to the* summa rudis, *who holds back the* hoplomachus *with his stick.*

times you are countering moves before you are consciously aware he's made them. At the end of it, your head is ringing from a blow to the helmet that came from nowhere, but you'd almost wrenched his shield away from his body, and he has to back off fast to avoid your killing strike.

You are vaguely aware of your teeth pulled right back across your gums and a kind of mounting berserker fury mounting within you. Is it possible you are enjoying this?

You follow up, and this time it's his turn to retreat. Every stab gets a block or evasion, every charge is countered; there seems no way through his guard. Yet he's moving backward, and you press him hard when he suddenly moves to attack, and there's a weakness in your sword shoulder, and your sword arm hardly works. You hammer desperately against his shield once more, and you hear a cry of pain as something gives, and he drops his shield. Yet you have to do the same, and smoothly do a practised switch to fight holding your sword left-handed, using your almost useless padded sword arm as a shield.

You're hard-hit and losing blood, but Priscus is in bad shape too. His chest is heaving, and he's in obvious pain. You're both in unusual territory here, because gladiators don't usually fight sword-to-sword, let alone right-hand against left. His attack is clumsy with fatigue, and you get in a slash at his throat that he blocks by dropping his head so that the sword bounces

from his helmet. He drops, stunned. You step forward to re-engage, and your knees go. Falling to the sand, you realize you are blacking out from blood loss. There's no choice but to extend a finger, and call on the umpires to stop the fight. Priscus floats into your blurring vision, and you note incredulously that his finger too has been raised in surrender. Then everything goes dark.

✣ ✣ ✣

Even as Priscus fought on, so too certainly did Verus
And for that long time the battle was close-fought
The crowd repeatedly called for both to stand down
But Caesar obeyed his own law
and that law was to keep going with the shield
until a finger was raised
What he could do, he did, allocating dishes and prizes for each
But equal they stayed until the end
Equal in the fight, equally they yielded
Caesar gave the wooden sword and the palm to both
The prize of skill for courage.

MARTIAL ON *THE SPECTACLES* 29

✣ ✣ ✣

Codex Gladiorum

At the opening of the Flavian Amphitheatre Titus had 9,000 beasts killed: 5,000 wild and 4,000 domesticated.

✛

Augustus seemed particularly to have it in for African animals. He says he killed off 3,500 animals in 'African beast hunts' including, by another source, 36 crocodiles.

✛

Like most Romans, gladiators are organized into either collegia (guilds) or burial clubs, so losers can generally expect a decent burial and perhaps a tombstone.

✛

An *essedarius* (chariot fighter) called Parius once received such massive applause that Caligula stormed from the imperial box in a jealous rage, complaining bitterly that the Romans thought more of a gladiator than their emperor.

✛

According to his biographer Suetonius, the emperor Titus would often exchange badinage with spectators about his favoured fighters.

✛

Drusus, son of the emperor Tiberius, was fond of lethal gladiator bouts, so much so that his father rebuked him that the really sharp swords he favoured had become known as 'Drusians'.

✛

Just as *habet* signifies that a gladiator has been hit, the cry of *practum est* ('that's done it') indicates a killing blow.

✛

Augustus, always keen on *romanitas* (the art of being distinctively Roman), insisted that spectators at the games wear togas.

✛

IX

Death and Other Alternatives to Retirement

Reputation? It's soon forgotten. Applauding hands are empty.

MARCUS AURELIUS *MEDITATIONS* 4.3

✢ ✢ ✢

A badly-wounded gladiator is not normally put down as though he were an injured animal, though an exception may be made for an individual past saving who has been sentenced to die by the sword in any case. But – assuming he has won his fight or received a *missio* – any other mortally-wounded gladiator will receive the same degree of palliative care as a legionary might expect in similar circumstances. This may give a dying gladiator the chance to say goodbye to his loved ones and check that his dues to his funeral club are paid up to date.

Consequently, for a gladiator to awaken in the Saniarum after a bout is by no means the worse thing that can happen. For a start, the best medical care in the empire is now available to assist with his recovery. Secondly, the fact that he was not finished off by Charun's hammer in the arena while unconscious suggests that the gladiator has at least a fighting chance of recovery. Thirdly, it means that he either won his bout, or acquitted himself with enough distinction that the crowd voted for him to live. To all these reasons for optimism can be added the healthy satisfaction of having beaten the odds yet again.

As a very rough guide, the chances of an average gladiator coming out of a fight alive are about five to one in his favour. As an average gladiator will fight two or three times a year, he can expect to be dead two years into his contract. Therefore, paradoxical as it may seem, the longer a gladiator has been fighting, the better his chances of survival. This is because there is in fact no such thing as an 'average' gladiator. Every gladiator is an individual, and his personal chances depend on his circumstances, his skill, and above all, his luck.

✢ ✢ ✢

*To the departed spirit of Urbicus, a primus palus secutor…who lived
22 years and fought 13 times. To a well-deserving husband from Laurica, his
wife of seven years, and also from Olympias the five-month-old daughter
he left behind, and her [slave?] Fortunensis.
Take this warning, and kill whom you vanquish, and may his fans cherish
his departed spirit.*

GLADIATOR TOMBSTONE *ILS* 5115 MILAN

✢ ✢ ✢

The truly endangered species is Gladiator Tironis, those taking their first steps
into the game. A lot depends on where
and when they fight, but at a rough esti-
mate slightly over half of all beginners
fail to make it through their first year.
(Though, as they say, your first fight may
be dangerous, but your last fight is the
one that gets you.) No one really keeps
score of survival averages, and wandering through a gladiator cemetery doesn't
tell the full story, because it is the more
durable class of gladiator who picks up
enough money to afford a tombstone,
and dependents who care enough to
raise one.

- -

*The funeral stele of Urbicus (translated
above). The inference appears to be that
Urbicus passed up the chance to kill an
opponent in a fight – but the favour was
not returned in a later rematch.*

The sweet palm of victory. The Thracian Satornius of Smyrna looks excusably smug as he watches the tips from the audience pile up after a winning bout.

- -

✠ ✠ ✠

To the departed spirit of Marcus Antonius Niger, veteran Thracian[-style gladiator] who fought 18 times and lived 38 years. Flavia Diogenes made this monument for her well-deserving husband at her own expense.

GLADIATOR TOMBSTONE *ILS* 5090 ROME

✠ ✠ ✠

Things were better 100 years ago, when the Augustan decrees forbade combats to the death, and fights with edged weapons were relatively rare. These days, with the crowd ever more thirsty for extravagant fights and bloodshed, mortality rates are higher. All of the following factors affect an individual's chances:

Frequency The more often a gladiator fights, the more he is at risk. Fighting at frequent intervals causes considerable psychological and emotional stress, and too many appearances in quick succession mean that a gladiator loses the essential edge that might make the difference between life and death.

Infrequency A gladiator who has not fought for a while is just as much at risk against an in-form gladiator as one who has fought once too often.

Popularity If a gladiator loses his fight, his chances of survival drop dramatically – and that's assuming he lasts long enough to throw himself on the mercy of the crowd. His best bet is to make the spectators believe he has fought well enough to provide more entertainment in a future engagement.

The authorities A man sentenced to die by the sword will so die, and the odds against him will rise as his 'use by' date approaches. However, there's no appeal and little chance if a *lanista* has decided, for whatever reason, that any particular gladiator is better off dead. (For example, if the *lanista* has been paid off by an influential husband who has found out about his wife's late-night training sessions.)

Fortuna and Nemesis Above all, the opinion of these two ladies is paramount. Not for nothing do gladiators revere Fortune and Fate. Every fighter has at some time gambled on a feint, made a lucky guess as to an opponent's intentions, or made a wild parry that somehow blocked a fatal blow. You'll find statues to these two goddesses at many training schools and arenas, and with good reason.

The goddess Fortuna, known to later generations as Lady Luck. A wise gladiator will visit her temple frequently.

✛ ✛ ✛

*To the spirits of the departed, Glauco of Mutina fought seven times, and
perished on the eighth. He lived 23 years and five days. Aurelia and those
who loved him set this [memorial] up to her well-deserving husband. Find
your own fortune, and do not trust Nemesis, for that is how I was fooled.*

GLADIATOR TOMBSTONE *CIL* 5.3466

✛ ✛ ✛

Most gladiators will, sooner or later, die on the sand. There are two ways to
avoid this:

- The easiest – though it is far from easy – is simply to fight through until the
completion of service, and obtain the *rudis*, the wooden sword that tells
the world that a gladiator has completed the terms of his contract and can
retire from the arena.

- Or (and this is in the hands of Fortuna), a gladiator may receive a wound
debilitating enough to prevent him fighting further, yet which is not
lethal. It is to prevent this very eventuality that most gladiators are
armoured for protection against all but lethal wounds.

*A medicus patches up a thigh
wound. The patient endures
the treatment more stoically
than his son.*

*This mosaic reminds us that the average gladiator's pension plan may
need to be switched to a funeral fund at a moment's notice.*

A gladiator who has been hard hit, yet survives, will get the best physiotherapy available, with the hope that he can be presented again in the arena.
Even a slightly crippled gladiator of no renown might find himself back
fighting with the *gregarii*, those low-class gladiators who fight in packs. A
famous gladiator who can fight no more might find himself a place in the
school as a *doctor*, instructing trainees – not least in how to avoid the
mistake which ultimately got him stabbed. Occasionally there may be a rare
gladiator who is, for example, badly wounded in the shoulder of his sword
arm. If he is a relative beginner yet has enough money from tips from the
crowd, or even as a gift from the emperor as reward for a well-fought fight,
he may be able to purchase a release from his contract.

✢ ✢ ✢

Asiaticus, primus palus, released after 53 victories ...

CIL 12.5837

What next?

A gladiator who has been released by the *ludus* has to make a number of adjustments. A veteran might need to spend some time becoming de-institutionalized. Brutal and spartan as the *ludus* is, life there has compensations. A gladiator does not have to worry where the next meal is coming from, or who will provide heating for his room and clothing for his back. Yet if he has planned well, the veteran has a wife, and perhaps a family, waiting for him, and a clear plan in mind for what happens next.

Immediate steps

It is highly unlikely that a gladiator who has survived until retirement will be allowed to slip unremarked from the life of the *ludus*. Such a man is an iconic figure to the younger gladiators, an example they can aspire to emulate. Expect the *lanista* to put on some form of ceremony for the retiree, with as imposing a high-ranking figure as his contacts can arrange to present the *rudis* in as public a ceremony as possible. Industrial quantities of alcohol may be consumed.

✦ ✦ ✦

Four brothers pleaded with [the emperor] Claudius for the discharge of their father, an essedarius [chariot fighter]. To huge public applause, Claudius presented the man with the customary wooden sword.

SUETONIUS *LIFE OF CLAUDIUS* 21

✦ ✦ ✦

As soon as he is able once more to walk in a straight line, the retiring gladiator is well-advised to head for a temple, perhaps the Pantheon on the edge of the Campus Martius, and there give thanks to the gods for his survival. Pay particular attention to Nemesis, for though the hazards of the arena are past, life in Rome can never be taken for granted, and fate's handmaiden requires her due.

With these wise precautions taken, the ex-gladiator can enjoy the novel sensation of actually expecting to survive for the next few years.

Career options

A gladiator, retired or not, is an *infamis*, a person of low repute, and will remain so until he dies. The stain of *infamia* restricts many of his public rights, though he retains the legal safeguards of a private individual. Thus he can act for himself in business or in the courts, but doing so on another's behalf is frowned on in the first instance and strictly forbidden in the latter. Going into politics is out of the question. Interestingly, a gladiator becomes *infamis* as soon as he takes money to appear in a fight. Just as men and women can take a string of lovers and avoid *infamia* right up to the moment they are paid for their services, a gladiator loses his right to respectability the moment he prostitutes his fighting skills. On top of legal restrictions, an ex-gladiator's career options are limited by the applications to which his highly specialized skills can be turned.

✛ ✛ ✛

Beryllus…a Greek, freed after his 20th combat…

GLADIATOR TOMBSTONE *CIL* 12.3323

✛ ✛ ✛

Bodyguard There's nothing like having a recognized killer standing at one's shoulder to keep the opposite parties coolly rational during a tense business negotiation, so gladiators, both retired and off-duty, are prime candidates for this role. A retired gladiator is a better choice for a wealthy Roman travelling abroad, especially for journeys through bandit-infested country, or simply along roads where the local yokels might consider an unescorted traveller fair game. While their general disposition and training make gladiators a poor choice for a military career (and the legions would turn up their noses at an *infamis* anyway), a gladiator is truly formidable at less organized types of mayhem, and we have seen that at least one commander has used his personal gladiators to keep unruly legionaries in check.

However, as we have seen, in the Republic, gladiatorial bodyguards could be found even in the forum in Rome.

Trainer As mentioned, a *ludus* might like to keep a veteran gladiator within the *familia*, because he is both an example and an inspiration to younger gladiators. Not only is the retiree living proof that it is possible to survive one's contract, but also the man might be persuaded to pass on some tips as to how others might achieve his status. Whether he takes a place at the *ludus* depends on what other options are available and how well he gets on with the *lanista*. There is, in fact, no reason why a gladiator cannot go on to become a *lanista* in his turn, though they are, if anything, regarded with even more contempt than gladiators.

Freelance Oddly enough, not all ex-gladiators want to be shot of the arena. Sometimes the draw of gladiatorial combat is just as strong for those who fight as it is to the crowds who watch. It is hard for one who has been the darling of cheering crowds to drop into quiet obscurity, while for others it is simply an urge to again feel as intensely alive as only a person in mortal danger can. Further, there is the fact that gladiators are not particularly good money managers, and even those who swore never to pick up a sword again are sometimes faced with the choice of dying insolvent or killing someone else as a wealthy man. *Editores* putting on a show may consider spectacular sums well-spent if they can get a famous name back on to the sand once more, and gladiators with nothing but their names and their blood to sell are sometimes happy to make the trade.

Business If a gladiator has hoarded his winning bonuses and wisely invested his tips from the crowd after each bout, he might have a handy nest egg to put into a small business. It helps that commerce in Rome can be a rough affair, in which violence and intimidation are far from unknown. The right businessman may well excuse a lack of business acumen or contacts if someone can bring to the partnership both financial assets and an ability to cope with any rough stuff. In some trades, such as innkeeping, a sufficiently famous gladiator might be required to do little more than occupy a seat and let people buy him drinks in exchange for a yarn or two.

However, apart from the risk to his liver, a retiree must remember that fame is fleeting with the fickle Roman public, and the hero of the arena just a few years ago can now walk unremarked down to the market. Best, then, to use the few years of one's fame as the foundation to build a solid business that can stand on its own merits.

In years to come no one may remember how the owner of a prosperous tavern on the lower slopes of the Caelian Hill acquired the wooden sword that hangs over his door. Nor will they understand why, when the shouting of the crowd at the Colosseum is carried by the wind up the valley, the old man smiles ruefully and touches the wound that withered his arm. Only he will remember what it was like to walk the sands of the arena and fight for his life as a gladiator of Rome.

✣ ✣ ✣

To the departed spirit of Alkibiades, dearest son…his devoted parents
raised this memorial… (Side A)
To the departed spirit of Julia Procula, well-deserving wife, Gaesus,
veteran murmillo, has made this memorial. (Side B)

TOMBSTONE *CIL* 6.10176

✣ ✣ ✣

It's Verus, back from Rome!
So how did you spend your years
in the big city?

Codex Gladiorum

Inscriptions from Trajan's time suggest that some gladiators appeared at the Colosseum for multiple successive fights during the victory games after the Dacian wars.

✢

The last gladiator fights at the Colosseum were in the AD 430s.

✢

Animal hunts at the Colosseum continued up to and beyond the end of the Roman empire in the west.

✢

In the 12th century the Colosseum was the family fortress of Rome's Frangipane clan.

✢

In the 13th century the Colosseum was damaged by a strong earthquake.

✢

During the 15th century the Colosseum was used as a stone quarry by locals – and indeed most of the structural damage by earth tremors is minor compared to human activity.

✢

In the 16th century the Pope (Sixtus V) considered demolishing the building altogether.

✢

The Colosseum survived because in the 17th century it was believed Christians were martyred there, though there is no evidence that this ever happened.

✢

The papal Good Friday procession starts beside the Colosseum.

✢

From the 18th century onwards, there have been systematic efforts to restore the building.

✢

Today, to show their opposition to the death penalty, the Italian authorities turn the lighting of the Colosseum at night from white to gold whenever a prisoner anywhere in the world is reprieved from death row.

✢

Nota bene: if you don't remember that a shield is also an offensive weapon, you won't make it to retirement.

Boundary of the Roman Empire in *c.* AD 180–200

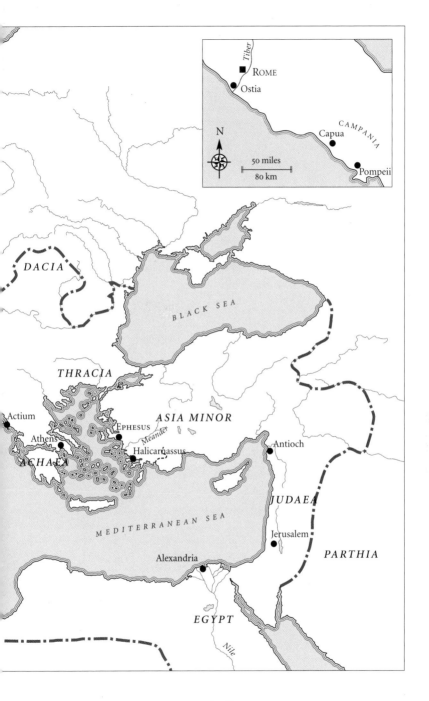

Glossary

These terms relate to the language of the arena. In everyday Latin, some words (such as *eques* and *magister*) have different meanings.

aedile a kind of magistrate in Rome responsible for staging games

andabata (plural *andabatae*) a special type of gladiator who fights blindfolded

auctoratus (plural *auctorati*) a free man who signs on as a gladiator

balteus metal belt worn by gladiators

cardiophylax breastplate

cena libera a last supper for the condemned

damnati the condemned (see pp 9–10 for the different types)

dimachaerus a gladiator who fights with two swords and no shield

doctor (plural *doctores*) a gladiator instructor

editor (plural *editores*) organizer of the games

eques (plural *equites*) a gladiator who fights on horseback with lance and short sword

essedarius (plural *essedari*) a chariot fighter

familia a 'family' of gladiators who live and train together

fasces bundle of rods and an axe carried by the *lictores*, which symbolize the state's authority to punish

fornices arches (like those outside the Flavian Amphitheatre, where the prostitutes ply their trade)

galerus armour protecting the shoulder and neck

gladius sword

greave a rigidly armoured knee-high sock

gregarius (plural *gregarii*) a gladiator who takes part in group combats

'*habet!*' he's been hit (as if he needed to be told)

harenarii arena slaves

hoplomachus a type of lightly-armed gladiator based on the Greek hoplite

infamis (plural *infames*)
  someone officially
  defined as a low-life
'iugula!' kill! (what a losing
  gladiator does not want to
  hear from the crowd)
lanista (plural *lanistae*) the
  manager of a gladiator school
laquearius a type of *retiarius*
  who fights with a lasso (never
  very popular)
libellus (plural *libelli*) a poster
libertus a gladiator who has
  served his term and is a free man
lictores imperial offiicials
  and enforcers
ludus (plural *ludi*) where
  gladiators live and train
magister head coach (in the
  context of the *ludus*)
manica protective sleeve
medicus medical doctor
missio discharge from the arena
'mitte!' let him go, let him live
munera assiforana gladiator
  games costing less than
  30,000 *sestertii*
munus (plural *munera*)
  originally a duty, such as that to
  one's ancestors, discharged by
  holding funeral games. Later, a
  pretext to stage gladiatorial bouts
munerarius he who presents a
  munus

murmillo 'the fish man', a
  type of heavy gladiator with
  a distinctive crested helmet
noxi those condemned to
  death in the arena
paegniarii clowns, mock-
  gladiators
palus wooden post; target for
  ancient hackers wanting to
  improve their swordmanship
parmularii the 'small-shield
  fighters', i.e. the more lightly
  armed gladiators
pollice verso the emperor's signal
  to save or kill a defeated gladiator
pompa the march of the gladiators
'practum est!' that's done it (i.e. a
  killing blow has been struck)
primus palus leading gladiator
  in his speciality in the *ludus*
probatio armorum the
  inspection of weapons by the
  giver of the games
procurator a government official
provocator 'the challenger', a
  type of heavy gladiator
  who fights with a short sword
  and large shield
quaestus causa for the money
  (a despicable reason for doing
  anything – compare *virtus causa*)
retiarius (plural *retiarii*)
  net-fighter

rudis the wooden sword presented to a gladiator on his retirement

sacramentum gladiatorum the gladiators' oath

Samnite the oldest type of Roman gladiator, named for the Samnite people of Campania who were (eventually) conquered by Rome

saniarum gladiator hospital

scissor a rare type of gladiator, usually seen in the east, equipped with a armoured sleeve that terminates in a hook or multiple blade

scutarii 'shield-carriers', the heavily armoured types of gladiator

secundus palus the second highest-ranked gladiator in the *ludus*, after the *primus palus*

secutor a heavily-armed gladiator, usually the opponent of the *retiarius*

sestertius (plural *sestertii*) a coin; four *sestertii* = one *denarius*, or about a day's wages for a workman

spoliarum where a dead gladiator is stripped of his armour and prepared for burial

sportulae tokens for gifts, thrown into the crowd at the arena

summum choragium storage place for scenery and equipment used in the arena

Thracian a type of lightly-armed gladiator whose main weapon is the Thracian dagger

tirones tiros or beginners who have not fought in the arena

vestarius the man responsible for the gladiators' costumes

veteres gladiators who have been there, done that, got the mail shirt

virtus bravery combined with integrity

virtus causa by reason of courage/virtue (compare *quaestus causa*)

venator (plural *venatores*) an animal-fighter; somewhat unfairly regarded as a warm-up act to the gladiators

vomitoria the wide entrances and corridors through which the crowd spills in and out of the amphitheatre

Acknowledgments

As ever, my deepest thanks and gratitude to all those who have generously given of their time and expertise on this project. The R M R S (Roman Military Research Society) gave me useful pointers on armour and swordplay and the Britannia reenactment group supplied pictures of their fighters in action. But none were more helpful than the gladiators of Ludus Nemesis, particularly the awesomely knowledgeable Svenja Grosser (a.k.a Medusa) and her team. Adrian Goldsworthy read the text and provided sources for some of the quotes given, and the library at the University of British Columbia helpfully allowed me to take up residence while tracking down the rest. A final note of thanks to the medical practitioner (anonymous by his request) who did not turn me in to the authorities after being questioned in detail about how and where to best stab someone with an eighteen-inch sword.

Further Reading

Baker, A., *The Gladiator: The Secret History of Rome's Warrior Slaves*, Ebury Press, London 2002

Barton, C. A., *The Sorrows of the Ancient Romans: The Gladiator and the Monster*, Princeton University Press, Princeton 1993.

Beacham, R.C., *Spectacle: Entertainments of Early Imperial Rome*, Yale University Press, New Haven 1999

Carter, M., 'Gladiatorial Ranking and the "SC de Pretiis Gladiatorum Minuendis" (*CIL* II 6278 = *ILS* 5163)', *Phoenix*, 57, no. 1/2, 2003, pp 83–14

Coleman, K., 'Fatal charades: Roman executions staged as mythological enactments', *The Journal of Roman Studies*, 80 (1990), 44–73

Futrell, A., *Blood in the Arena: The Spectacle of Roman Power*, University of Texas Press, Austin 1997

Grant, M., *Gladiators*, Delacorte Press, New York 1967

Köhne, E. and Ewigleben, C., eds, *Gladiators and Caesars: The Power of Spectacle in Ancient Rome*, British Museum Press, London and University of California Press, Berkeley 2000

Kyle, D.G., *Spectacles of Death in Ancient Rome*, Routledge, London and New York 1998

Junkelmann, M., *Das Spiel mit dem Tod*, Philipp von Zabern, Mainz 2000

Matthews, R., *Age of the Gladiators: Savagery and Spectacle in Ancient Rome*, Arcturus, London 2003

Matyszak, P., *Ancient Rome on Five Denarii a Day*, Thames & Hudson, London and New York 2007

Meijer, F., *The Gladiators: History's Most Deadly Sport*, Thomas Dunne Books, New York and Souvenir, London 2005

Nosov, K., *Gladiator: Rome's Bloody Spectacle*, Osprey, Oxford and New York 2009

Poliakoff, M.B., *Combat Sports in the Ancient World: Competition, Violence and Culture*, Yale University Press, New Haven 1987

Shadrake, S., *The World of the Gladiator*, Tempus, Stroud 2005

Wiedemann, T., *Emperors and Gladiators*, Routledge, London 1992

Wisdom, S. and McBride, A., *Gladiator 100 BC – AD 200*, Osprey, Oxford 2001

Websites

http://www.ludus-nemesis.eu/en/index.html
The website of gladiators Medusa, Cerberus and friends, who appear in these pages.

http://www.romanarmytalk.com/rat/viewforum.php?f=12
The definitive web forum for discussing ancient combat sports.

http://www.unrv.com/culture/gladiator.php
A good summary of gladiators; other forums on this website discuss all aspects of Roman life and culture. (Where the author hangs out after hours.)

http://depthome.brooklyn.cuny.edu/classics/gladiatr/index.htm
Another look at gladiators, from a US academic perspective.

Sources of Quotations

All quotations in this book from ancient Roman sources were translated into English by the author. The sources from which the quotations come are given in the text, apart from those listed below.

Page 29
'Decimus Iunius Brutus put on the first display of gladiators…'
Livy *Periochae* 16.6

Page 32
'Those who fight and die for Rome' and 'nothing but the air of Italy and sunlight of Italy to call their own'
Plutarch Lives: *Tiberius Gracchus* 9

Page 67
'They exercise until they drop…'
Galen *Exhortation to the Study of the Arts* 4

Page 103
'He had the better missile troops…'
Appian *The Civil Wars* 5.33

Page 105
'He never appeared in public without them in their complete panoply of armour…'
Cicero *Letters to Quintus* 2.4

Page 108
'Old Baldy [Crassus] settled the whole business with…'
Cicero *Letters to Atticus* 1.16

Page 110
'Many call him a gladiator's son. I don't want to lie…'
Tacitus *Annals* 11.21

Abbreviations used in the text
CIL Theodor Mommsen *et al* (eds), *Corpus Inscriptionum Latinarum*, 17 volumes, Walter de Gruyter & Co, Berlin, 1863 –

ILS Hermann Dessau (ed.), *Inscriptiones Latinae Selectae*, 3 volumes, 1892 – 1916 (facsimile editions Bibliolife, 2009 –)

LGOG L. Robert, *Les Gladiateurs dans l'Orient Grec* (École des Hautes Études, fasc. 278), Librairie Champion, Paris, 1940

Sources of Illustrations

KEY   a = above   c = centre   b = below   l = left   r = right

Sword motifs pictured throughout the text are by Peter Inker © Thames & Hudson Ltd, London.

akg-images/Peter Connolly 70
Archaeological Museum, El Djem 8
Archaeological Museum, Tripoli 50, 153, 170–171
Archivio della Soprintendenza Archeologica, Rome 126
Associated Press 85
Bardo Museum, Tunis 82
Bignor Roman Villa 54
Britannia (www.durolitum.co.uk) 137, 138, 139, 141b, 142, 143, 144
British Museum, London 2, 27, 33, 45, 63, 72, 79a, 79b, 106, 109l, 115, 167, 184
Colchester & Essex Museum 55
Deutsches Archäologisches Institut, Rome 10
From Victor Duruy, *History of Rome and the Roman People*, vols I–V, London (1884) 17, 19, 37, 39, 43, 49b, 60, 62, 91, 96, 100, 119, 121, 125, 148, 177, 182
From Carlo Fontana, *L'Anfiteatro Flavio descritto e delineato* (1725) 130
Galleria Borghese, Rome 38, 169
Kunsthistorisches Museum, Vienna 64
Leicester Museum & Art Gallery 112b
Leptis Magna Museum, photo Marlies Wendowski, courtesy of Mark Merrony 86–87
Ludus Nemesis (www.ludus-nemesis.eu) 140, 141a
Metropolitan Museum of Art, New York 28
Musée de Lectoure, Gers 77l
Musée du Louvre, Paris 73a, 154
Musée Romain, Avenches 78c
Musei Capitolini, Rome 6, 110
Musei Vaticani, Rome 16, 102, 112a, 128

Museo Archeologico 'La Civitella', Chieti 78b
Museo Arqueologico Nacional, Madrid 83, 84
Museo Archeologico Nazionale, Naples 25b, 81a, 81b, 88, 111, 146–147, 176
Museo Archeologico Nazionale, Taranto 7
Musée Archéologique, Sousse 49a
Museo Civico, Foligno 118
Museo della Civiltà Romana, Rome 156
Museo Nazionale, Cerveteri 25a
Museo Nazionale, Rome 109r
Museo Nazionale delle Terme, Rome 94, 151
Museum van Oudheden, Leiden 175
From Fausto e Felice Niccolini, *Le case ed i monumenti di Pompeii disegnati e descritti* (1854) 1, 41, 61, 73b, 166
Ny Carlsberg Glyptotek, Copenhagen 22, 104
Palazzo della Cancelleria, Rome 36
From J.H. Parker, *The Flavian Amphitheatre*, London (1876) 131
Römerhalle, Bad Kreuznach, copyright INTERFOTO/Alamy 77b
Römermuseum, Augst 80, 178
Sezione epigrafica delle Civiche Raccolte Archeologiche e Numismatiche, Milan 174
From William Smith, *A Dictionary of Greek and Roman Antiquities*, vols I–II, London (1890) 107
Staatliche Landesbildstelle, Saarland 150, 155, 162
Staatliche Museen, Berlin 44, 77r
Uffizi, Florence, 14
From Francesco Paolo Maulucci Vivolo, *Pompeii: I Graffiti Figurati* (1993) 76, 95
H.G. Wells, *The Outline of History*, London (1930) 20
Württembergisches Landesmuseum, Stuttgart 78a

Index

Page numbers in *italics* refer to illustrations and captions